the
woodworker's
handbook

the
woodworker's
handbook

roger horwood

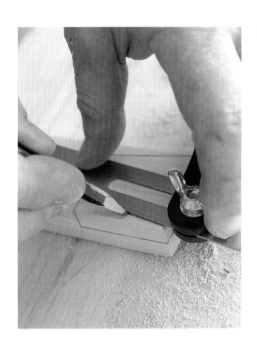

photography by ryno

NEW
HOLLAND

ACKNOWLEDGEMENTS

The author and publishers wish to thank the following companies and individuals for their assistance in putting this book together: For the generous loan of tools and equipment, and for sharing their knowledge and expertise, thank you to Mervin and Jakes at Feds DIY; The Hardware Centre; Allan Clack and Louise Ansell at The Paint & Waterproofing Centre; Anton at Rare Woods; Reinstein's Antiques/Furniture Restorers; and Mark Paulse at TickTin Timbers. We also wish to thank Sue McAdam at Loft Living for allowing us to use their premises for photographing the finished projects, and Dave Cresswell at Stevens & Co (Pty) Ltd for entrusting us with their Ryobi machinery. A very special word of thanks to Ross Badenhorst at Woodknot for his tireless efforts and fine craftmanship in making up the projects (excluding the turned table).

First published in 1999 by New Holland Publishers Ltd
London ❋ Cape Town ❋ Sydney ❋ Auckland

4 6 8 10 9 7 5 3

24 Nutford Place	14 Aquatic Drive
London W1H 6DQ	Frenchs Forest
United Kingdom	NSW 2086, Australia

80 McKenzie Street	218 Lake Road
Cape Town 8001	Northcote, Auckland
South Africa	New Zealand

Copyright © 1999 New Holland Publishers Ltd
Copyright © 1999 in text: Roger Horwood
Copyright © 1999 in photographs: Struik Image Library
Copyright © 1999 in illustrations: Struik Image Library

ISBN 1 85974 079 0 (hc)
ISBN 1 85974 225 4 (pb)

Editor: Joy Clack
Designer: Petal Palmer
Design assistant: Lellyn Creamer
Consultants: Jeff Day (United States), Rod Osmond (Australia)
Photographer: Ryno
Stylist: Sylvie Hurford, Leigh de Vries (Assistant)
Illustrator: Dave Snook
Proofreader & indexer: Brenda Brickman

Reproduction by Hirt & Carter Cape (Pty) Ltd
Printed and bound in Malaysia by Times Offset (M) Sdn. Bhd.

contents

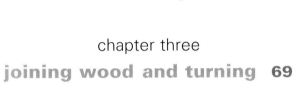

6 the woodworker's handbook

introduction

In the midst of the turmoil and stress of everyday life comes a lifeline – a book about fulfilment and enjoyment and working with a material that is a vital part and product of nature. Wood, with its beauty, strength and vast variety of colours, is probably the most ancient material with which humankind has worked. From sitting on a fallen log to rest, to the intricacies of filigree carving, wood has been an integral part of the history of mankind on every continent of the globe. In recent years, the pure enjoyment of working with wood as a hobby, rather than a commercial venture or convenient necessity, has flourished.

One of the wonderful things about working with wood is that, regardless of age, gender or any other consideration, almost anybody can become a proficient woodworker with a little patience and practice, and many people have derived years of joy from this delightful hobby.

Once you get the feel of the different tools and techniques described in this book, attain the basic woodworking skills outlined, and put these skills into practice on a few of the joints and relatively easy projects, then the sky's the limit! You can design your own projects and produce furniture, toys and other items of fine quality that will bring you the satisfaction of achievement as well as the benefit of years of practical use.

If you make your own furniture, there are economic benefits as well in that, not only will it be the size, design and quality you want, but it will also save you money.

The skill of successfully repairing broken furniture gives enormous satisfaction too, not only to yourself but to the friends who seek your help in this area.

chapter one

woods for the woodworker

Trees are alive! As unnecessary as it may seem to mention this, it is good to remember that wood is a product of nature and is therefore finite. Although many valiant efforts are being made to replant trees and preserve our forests, it would appear that we are fighting a losing battle as the availability of wood declines in the face of growing worldwide demand. It is not too difficult to replace the faster-growing trees that are ready for harvesting 20–25 years after planting, but what do you do about the beautiful hardwoods, many of which may take as long as 300 years to mature? Whenever you handle a beautiful piece of timber you should think of its history, appreciate the natural beauty of its finite resource and do your utmost not to waste what nature has taken so long to produce.

Let's take a closer look at the resource with which we will be working. A visit to a well-stocked timberyard is an adventure! First, the visitor will be impressed by the number of different types of wood available, and the variety of lengths and sizes in which it is presented. And then there is the olfactory experience – the variety of aromas exuded from woods is a pleasure in and of itself, and, in the writer's opinion, is better than a visit to any perfumery!

The different woods listed in this book fall into two major categories: **natural wood** (direct from the tree) and **man-made 'wood'** (manufactured from by-products of wood from the tree).

Natural wood

This category is divided into two major groups: softwoods and hardwoods. When applied to wood, the terms 'soft' and 'hard' are usually in relation to each other, but there are exceptions. Balsa, for example, is physically probably one of the softest woods available commercially, but due to its make-up, it is scientifically classified as a hardwood. Balsa is a light wood, both in weight and in colour, and has very little structural strength. It is not used for furniture making, but mainly in the construction of model aeroplanes and other such projects.

At the other end of the scale are hardwoods, such as teak and ironwood, which are amazingly strong, hard and durable.

There are literally hundreds of different natural woods and it is important that you select wood with the characteristics you require for the type of project you have in mind. This choice will be governed by factors such as durability, strength, practicality and colour. For example, most ordinary kitchen and children's furniture will be made from pine, as it is relatively inexpensive, easy to work, and it doesn't matter too much if it is abused through everyday use. On the other hand, dining-room and lounge furniture will usually be made from an attractive and relatively expensive hardwood, as it is important that the furniture is aesthetically pleasing as well as long-lasting.

The name of each wood represented in this chapter is, in most instances, the common name for a number of varieties within that species. Although it is possible to import almost any wood available on world markets, the type of wood you use within each group will largely depend on what is the easiest to obtain in your location.

SOFTWOODS

Softwoods are harvested from trees that take about 20–25 years to mature. The most prolific wood in this category comes from the family of trees known collectively as pine. Pine is available almost all over the world and is still relatively inexpensive. The trees grow tall and straight, a characteristic which, in years gone by, made them suitable for the masts of sailing vessels as well as large construction beams. Their long, uninterrupted growth makes pine trees perfect for use in the furniture and building industries.

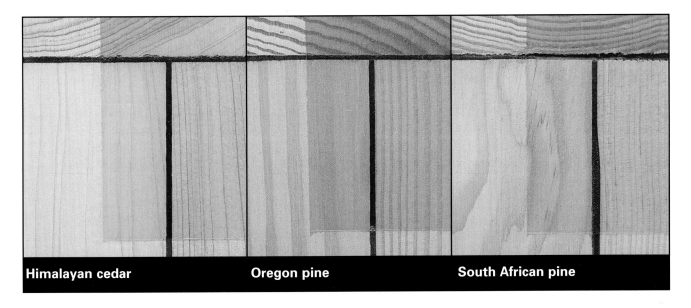

Himalayan cedar   Oregon pine   South African pine

Cedar
Generally the colour of liquid honey, most varieties of cedar are aromatic and have a straight, clearly defined grain. Western red cedar is often used in the construction of houses and joinery, while cedar of Lebanon is a popular choice for cabinet-making as its chemical make-up deters insects. Many varieties in the cedar family are not particularly strong, but they are very durable.

Oregon pine (Oregon cedar, Douglas fir)
Oregon pine is a popular wood used in country-style furniture. It is easy to work, has a particularly attractive grain and a lovely brown-yellow colour. This wood gives off a pleasant aroma when being worked.

Pine (all varieties)
Pine is generally a clean white or creamy yellow colour. It is easy to work, is in plentiful supply and is therefore usually inexpensive. Pine can be obtained in a variety of sizes, but good-quality, solid boards are not easy to come by. When selecting pine for furniture making, watch out for knots as they can be a feature or a problem. Knots in timber are caused by the growth of a branch out of the trunk and if they are 'dead' they can fall out of the board (literally!), but if they are 'live' they can be a very attractive feature in the finished product.

HARDWOODS

The woods in this category are harvested from trees that take a very long time to grow to maturity, in many cases as many as 200–300 years. Traditionally, the more popular hardwoods for woodworking include oak, beech, walnut and mahogany. Generally speaking, the hardwoods have a much more beautiful character, pattern and grain formation, and are far more hardy than the softwoods. They are, therefore, a more popular choice for furniture making than softwoods.

American red oak
This wood is heavy, durable and very strong. It has similar qualities to American white oak, but tends to be redder in colour and has a more interesting grain.

American white oak
Although similar in appearance to other oak varieties, American white oak has a yellowish-red colour and a less attractive grain. What it loses in attractiveness, however, it gains in a reputation for toughness and durability.

Australian red cedar
Unlike other cedar varieties, this timber is a hardwood. It is slightly redder in colour than other cedars and has a grain very similar in appearance to Oregon pine (see page 11) when finished. It is most commonly used for small cabinets and other furniture.

Beech
This is another popular furniture-making wood as it is light, strong and hard. The whiter the wood, the younger it is and the more popular for furniture making. Avoid using the darker or discoloured wood as this comes from much older trees and has the tendency to split quite easily.

Beech has an excellent texture, making for easy planing, joining and finishing. It takes the bumps and scrapes of normal household use very well, and because of its smooth finish it is also a favourite choice for use in tool handles.

Cherry
Cherry wood is a popular choice with professional cabinet-makers, but it is quite difficult to obtain and is usually expensive outside the USA and Canada.

It can be difficult to work as the grain tends to tear easily, but if worked properly it can give a very beautiful finish.

The two most commonly used species within this family are English cherry and American cherry.

Elm
This attractive timber is often used for making large pieces of furniture. It is a light red-brown in colour and some species, such as European elm, have a beautiful figure and burl pattern.

Iroko
Iroko is generally golden-brown in colour, and has a pungent and irritating aroma when worked in machines.

Similar to teak in appearance and durability, but not as oily, iroko is a good choice for outdoor furniture.

Jelutong
This light-yellow timber is often used as a substitute for South African yellowwood as its appearance and characteristics are very similar, but it is a great deal less expensive. Although strong and durable, boards need to be selected carefully because they have a tendency to contain oval holes, as well as circular worm holes.

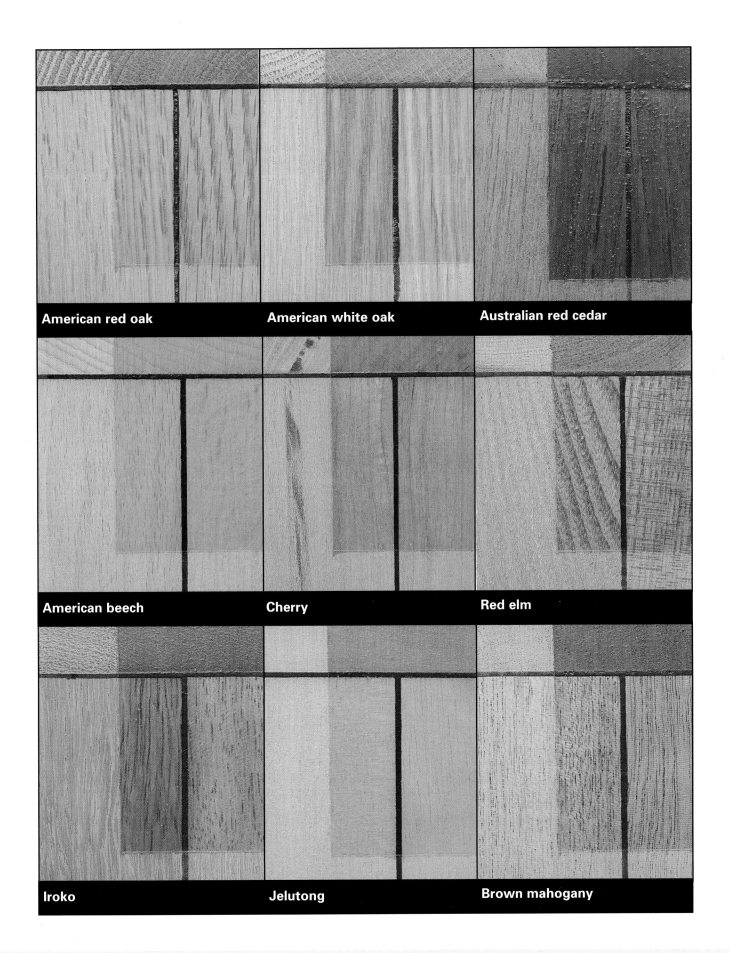

American red oak

American white oak

Australian red cedar

American beech

Cherry

Red elm

Iroko

Jelutong

Brown mahogany

White maple

Meranti

Oak

Vietnamese rosewood

Sapele

Sycamore

Burmese teak

Tulipwood

Walnut

Mahogany

This is a very beautiful timber with a red-brown colour and a distinctive grain. Most varieties are quite heavy in comparison to other woods, and they are strong and durable. Although it is a popular choice for furniture-making, and has been for many years, mahogany, particularly the Spanish and St Domingo varieties, is becoming more scarce and expensive, mainly due to high demand.

Maple

There are many varieties of maple, but generally it has a very light-brown colour with an attractive grain that finishes well. It is a tough wood and versatile for all aspects of woodworking.

One particularly pretty variety is bird's-eye maple, which has regular dark-brown markings that look like its name suggests. Bird's-eye maple is often used for small-scale woodworking projects such as presentation boxes, and veneers.

Meranti

Meranti is very similar in many ways to mahogany. It is a plain but attractive straight-grained hardwood with a reddish colour. Because of its straight and even grain, meranti is most often used in the construction of door and window frames and for skirting boards.

When working this wood keep a pair of tweezers in your workshop as more splinters end up in fingers and hands from meranti than any other kind of timber!

Oak (all species except American varieties)

This very beautiful hardwood is grown in many parts of the world and the type of oak you use will depend upon where you live. Oak is a popular choice for lounge and dining-room furniture and tends to darken with age. It is an amazingly strong wood which, in days gone by, was used in the construction of ships. It was sawn into massive beams for the construction of houses (typically in the Elizabethan period) that can still be seen in Britain to this day – testimony to its longevity!

Rosewood

There are many varieties of rosewood available. This species takes it name from the aroma of the wood – the underground section of canary rosewood is, in fact, used in the preparation of perfume. Rosewood has a dark-red to red-brown colour and finishes beautifully. It is used for showpieces of furniture, pianos, veneers and turned bowls.

Sapele (sapele mahogany)

This very grainy and coarse-textured wood is mainly used as a veneer on manufactured boards, and is popularly used in this form for making pianos and other furniture. It is red-brown in colour, strong and durable, but has a rather dull appearance. Most varieties originate from West Africa.

Sycamore

This is a beautiful wood when finished, if you can get it to that stage, as it does not take well to seasoning or to changes in climatic conditions. This wood is compact, has a fine grain and can be worked quite easily. It usually has a light-cream to white colour, but tends to darken with age.

Sycamore is commonly used for in the making of violins and general furniture, but beware of warping and shrinkage.

Teak

This straight-grained, heavy, but particularly durable wood has a greasy feel to it that is caused by its high oil content. It is suitable for outdoor furniture, deck planks and shipbuilding, although the oiliness makes the use of wood glue a little tricky. Light-brown to burnt-gold in colour, it is a classically beautiful wood to work and gives a lovely finish, but it tends to be hard on blades.

Tulipwood

This beautifully striped, very hard wood, erroneously referred to as poplar, is a light red-brown in colour and finishes well. It is often used for turning and decorative purposes, but is not a common choice for pieces of furniture.

Walnut

Walnut is an exquisitely beautiful hardwood with a dark-brown, grey or red colour. This wood is a pleasure to work and a joy to see. Unfortunately, due to high demand, it is becoming quite expensive and is therefore only used for small projects, for example in the production of high-quality gun stocks.

'MAN-MADE' WOODS

There are a number of reasons why it is necessary to manufacture 'man-made' woods, and among these is the fact that natural wood is becoming more and more scarce and increasingly expensive. Another factor is that large, natural-wood boards tend to warp, whereas 'man-made' boards are much more stable. Built-in kitchen and bedroom units, in particular, would be very difficult and prohibitively expensive to produce in natural wood.

Medium-density fibreboard (MDF)

This board is manufactured by reducing wood to a very fine fibre, mixing it with resin and then compressing it under pressure to form sheets. Standard sizes and thicknesses vary from country to country, with 12 mm (½ in) or the closest available thickness being the most suitable for general furniture-making. Your local hardware store or woodyard should be able to supply sheets of almost any size you require. This wood has a very smooth finish, which can be hand- or spray-painted, and is also very versatile as it can be routed and shaped relatively easily. In blocks thick enough, it also turns remarkably well!

Plywood

In woodworking, there is often a need for relatively thin boards that have a high strength-to-weight ratio, for example panels in doors or cabinets, and drawer bottoms. This is where plywood comes into its own. It is made by laminating thin sheets of wood so that the grain of each sheet is at right angles to the one adjacent to it.

Plywood is usually produced in sheets of 2.44 m (8 ft) by 1.22 m (4 ft) and in a variety of thicknesses, ranging from a very thin three-ply (about 3 mm/⅛ in thick) to multi-ply (about 25 mm/1 in thick). Your local woodyard should have any dimensions you require.

Although the surface is not as smooth as MDF, plywood has a natural-wood appearance and is far stronger than MDF.

Blockboard (copine, pre-glued panels)

While long, wide boards of natural wood can be unstable, there is still a demand for them. To meet this demand the timber industry has come up with the solution of gluing together strips of pine or oak, which are about 35 mm wide (1⅜ in) and 6–22 mm (¼–⅞ in) thick, to form boards up to 700 mm (28 in) wide. Blockboard, while being very strong and stable, retains the appearance of natural wood.

Boards are manufactured in a variety of widths and lengths, up to about 700 mm (28 in) wide by up to 4 m (13 ft) long and usually in a standard thickness of 22 mm (⅞ in).

Chipboard

Similar in some ways to MDF, chipboard is made by mixing wood chips with resin and then compressing it under pressure to form sheets of similar size and thickness to MDF. This is not a satisfactory wood for furniture-making and household projects as it does not finish very well, splits easily on the end grain and seems to be especially hard on saw blades. It can, however, be used where the surface will not be visible, for example in the construction of upholstered furniture.

Veneered chipboard

Veneered chipboard looks and finishes better than plain chipboard. Mass-produced furniture is often made from this material, but because of its unattractive end grain, it should be avoided for furniture-making and household use.

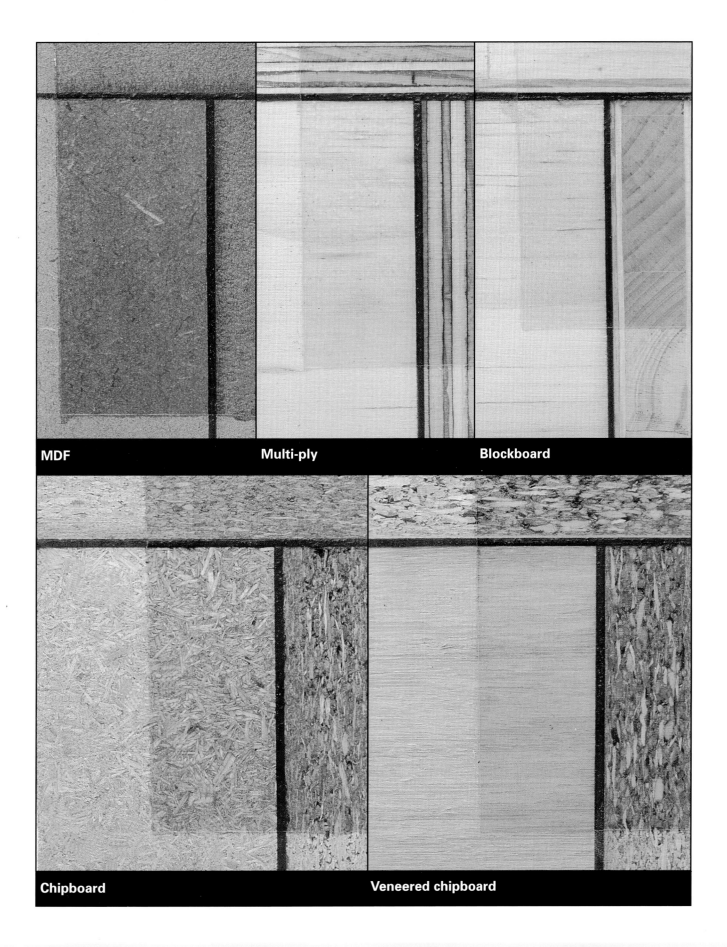

MDF

Multi-ply

Blockboard

Chipboard

Veneered chipboard

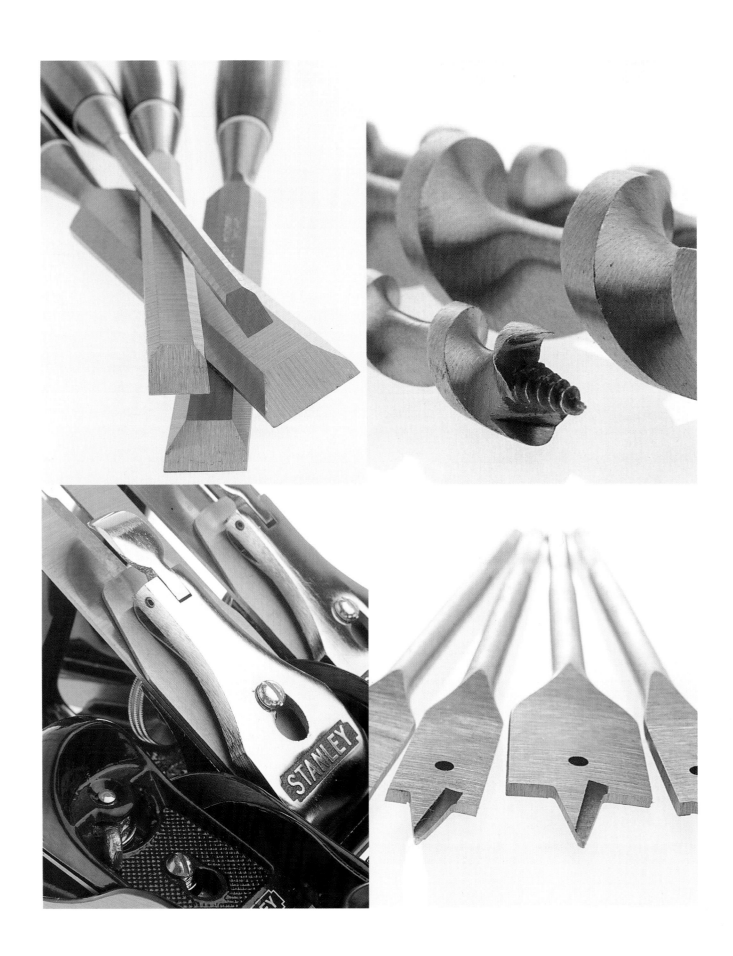

tools for the job

You don't need to spend a fortune on tools to achieve satisfactory results – even a small set of basic tools can be used to produce good quality, albeit relatively simple pieces of furniture. If money is a problem, first buy the essentials and then gradually build up a comprehensive set of tools. One important maxim is 'buy good – buy once'. A good quality, expensive tool will usually last a lifetime if properly cared for, whereas a cheap, poor quality tool probably won't do the job effectively and may break after a short time. A quality tool becomes part of you as you use it. You become familiar with its weight and the feel of it, and the more you use it, the more adept you will become at perfecting even the most difficult woodworking techniques.

Noise control

As most woodworkers tend to practise their hobby at home, either in a garage or in a workshop attached to the house, it is important to be aware of noise control.

Woodworking machinery has the tendency to be very noisy and although this would be acceptable in industrial areas, in a suburban situation it can cause considerable inconvenience to neighbours. It is therefore important to select the days and times when you wish to practise your hobby in order to avoid undue disturbance, together with the possible ensuing problems.

It is also a good idea to take simple soundproofing precautions, such as keeping workshop windows and doors closed when the weather and environment will permit it and, if you're planning to build a workshop, make sure that it's in a suitable location as far as your neighbours are concerned.

Another disadvantage of the noise factor is that it can affect the woodworker physically. Continuous exposure to noisy machinery can result in irreversible damage to the highly sensitive middle and inner parts of your ears, and it is strongly advised never to switch on a machine before putting on industrial ear protectors (see page 55).

The two most important factors to consider when choosing a workbench are the stability and the height. Stability is essential as it is unacceptable to have a piece of wood moving about, even by a fraction, when you're trying to plane or drill accurately. Height is another very important feature. If the bench is too low, working will become difficult and the continuous bending over can result in backache. Alternatively, if the bench is too high, the work surface will be too close to your face and this again makes for uncomfortable and unsatisfactory working conditions.

If you buy a commercially produced workbench and find that it's too high or too low, either cut a suitable length off the legs or add a block to extend each leg to bring the work surface to the required, comfortable height.

Freestanding bench

This bench is typical of commercially manufactured woodworking benches that are custom-made for the job, but although satisfactory, they can be expensive. Features will differ from one manufacturer to another, so it's a good idea to investigate as many models as possible before making your choice. A freestanding bench has the advantage of being portable (although it can be heavy) and allows freedom of movement right around the bench. One of the few disadvantages is that if you have a confined working area, such as a garage, it can be a nuisance to have to drag the bench into your working area each time you need to use it.

If you can tackle a job of this size, a good practical exercise is to design and build your own bench. This has the advantage of being less expensive and will give you the pleasure of producing your own bench with its own design features.

This typical example of a freestanding carpenter's workbench includes features such as a fitted bench vice with large and efficient jaws, and a drawer for tools or odds and ends.

Fixed bench

This bench is ideal for an area with restricted work space, but it is not commercially available. You need to be careful where you select your site for fixing, as once one is fixed in place it cannot be moved. Choose a position with ample natural light or install a flourescent light directly above the work surface. Since leaving school I have never worked on a commercially manufactured bench, always preferring to make my own and fix it to the garage wall. Again there are the advantages of being able to design the bench to suit your own length, width and height requirements, and it also allows you to position attachments, such as a bench vice and stops, where you want them to be.

The surface can be made from boards joined with a biscuit joint (see page 91), but these boards need to be fairly sturdy and at least 30 mm (1¼ in) thick. If you do not envisage any heavy work, then a chipboard surface should be adequate – it's certainly cheaper than solid wood but not nearly as satisfactory in the final analysis.

The supports and legs must also be sturdy (at least 50 x 90 mm/2 x 3½ in), with a wooden or metal bracket for extra strength. A halving (lap) joint (see pages 80–81) is adequate for the join between the leg and the support beam, and the support beam and the wall beam.

The wall support beam, which should be the same length as the bench, needs to be firmly screwed or bolted to the wall with the aid of masonry plugs. The work surface boards can then be screwed to the support beams. Remember to leave a sufficient overlap at the front and ends of the bench to allow free movement around the three sides of the bench without stubbing your toes on the legs, as well as space for the use of G-clamps (see page 41) when securing work to the surface.

Collapsible benches

These commercially produced benches have some distinct advantages and disadvantages over the previous two described. The advantages are that it is collapsible and therefore highly portable and takes up very little storage space when collapsed. It also provides a solid and stable work surface when in use and the whole work surface acts as a vice.

The main disadvantage of this kind of bench is that the work surface area is very small and often too low to provide comfortable working conditions.

A woodworker's bench vice should be fitted to the front of the bench with its wooden jaws flush with the work surface.

The bench vice

If you make your own bench, the choice of a bench vice is very important. Make sure that you purchase a woodworking vice and not one designed for metalwork. Bolt the vice to the bench, usually near the left-hand end, with the top of the jaws level with the surface of the bench.

A collapsible workbench such as this one can be used where workshop space is restricted, or as a complementary workbench to a larger fixed one.

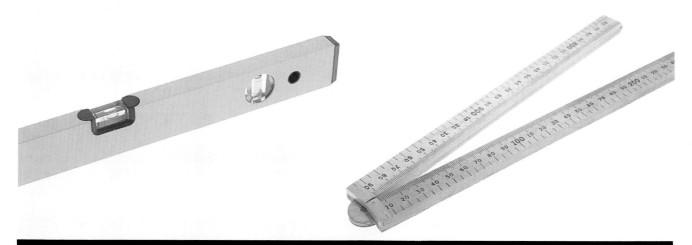

Spirit level (mason's level)

Wooden rule

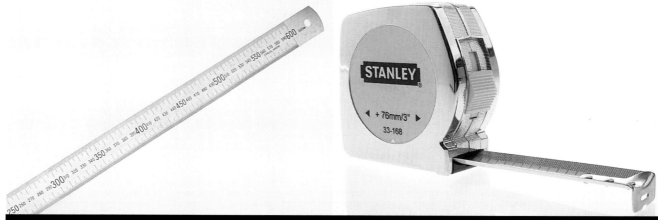

Steel rule

Retractable steel tape measure

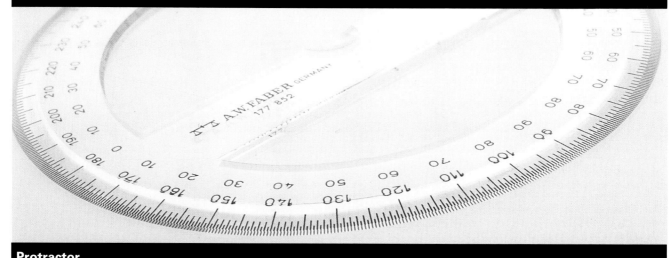

Protractor

Every woodworking job requires measurements to be made, so measuring devices are essential to the woodworker. The type of tool you select and use will depend upon the application, cost and accuracy of the tool, as well as personal preference. One rule (no pun intended!) of woodworking is 'measure twice, cut once'. Considerable frustration and additional expense can be avoided by checking for a second time that the required measurement is accurately marked on the wood. A simple example of how this would work in practice is that when cutting a piece of wood to length, the woodworker will often measure and mark the distance, draw in the square line across the wood and then commence the saw cut. It is strongly advised that once the square lines have been drawn, the distance is measured a second time to ensure accuracy.

As unlikely as it may seem, tapes and rules may vary in their accuracy from one to another. It is therefore advisable to use the same measuring device throughout a job as the possibility exists of some very strange deviations occurring!

Spirit level (mason's level)
This tool is usually made of a straight piece of wood or metal with a rectangular glass section filled with oil. The oil has a bubble suspended in it, which should maintain a central position between two marked lines to indicate when the level is resting in an exact horizontal or vertical position.

Even though spirit levels are most commonly used for bricklaying, they can also be used in woodworking to double-check that a surface is level, particularly for larger projects, such as a table.

Wooden rule
This is the woodworker's traditional measuring instrument. It has four distinct fold-out sections with brass ends, which are joined together with brass hinges. The rule itself is made from hardwood and is marked out in imperial (inches) or metric (millimetres); some makes have both. The wooden carpenter's rule does have some disadvantages, however, in that it can be broken quite easily and its edges can be damaged through regular use, affecting the accuracy of your measurement. It can also be quite a clumsy tool to use and has largely been replaced by the steel rule and retractable steel tape measure.

Steel rule
The steel rule is much more versatile and durable than its wooden counterpart. It is not easily damaged and therefore the markings, which may be metric, imperial or both, remain intact, making it a very accurate instrument to use.

It has another advantage over the wooden rule in that it can be used as a cutting guide, as a knife can be drawn along the edge of the rule without causing any damage.

Retractable steel tape measure

This has probably become the most widely used measuring tool for the general woodworker and hobbyist. It has several advantages over the two rules mentioned above, as it is more compact, it is capable of measuring greater distances (anything from 3–5 m/10–16 ft), and it can be used for inside measurements where a steel or wooden rule may be too cumbersome to fit into the space available. As with the other rules it may be marked out in imperial, metric or both. Its major disadvantage is that the tape is quite flimsy and must be used carefully to obtain an accurate measurement.

Protractor

A protractor is used to establish and set angles, but as the general woodworker is unlikely to need to do this very often, a simple, inexpensive plastic protractor such as is used in schools should be suitable for most projects. Bear in mind, however, that the larger the protractor, the more accurate the measurements are likely to be.

GAUGES

It is often necessary to mark a continuous line on a piece of wood. While this is difficult to accomplish with an ordinary rule, special tools that can be fixed at a specific distance have been designed. For general woodworkers, only two gauges are necessary. These tools are nearly always made of wood, with the sliding stock secured by some form of thumbscrew.

Marking gauge

This tool is most often used for marking the width of a board from one prepared straight edge. A sharpened steel pin is used to score the surface of the wood, leaving a slight indentation. Once this line has been correctly marked, a sharp pencil can be drawn down the indentation to make it more visible.

The distance from the stock to the tip of the pin can be set using a steel or wooden rule. When this distance is almost correct, tighten the thumbscrew only part of the way and tap the stem of the gauge until the exact distance can be set. Once in place, tighten the thumbscrew.

Mortise gauge

The main difference between this gauge and the marking gauge is that the mortise gauge has two steel pins. This can be purchased as a separate tool, but is more often available as a combination mortise and marking gauge.

As the name suggests, this tool is used for marking out the mortise for a mortise and tenon joint. The steel pin furthest from the stock is fixed while the steel pin nearer to the stock is attached to a slide, allowing the distance between the two pins as well as the distance from the stock to the pins to be adjusted.

The distance between the two pins is usually set to the width of the mortise chisel you intend to use (this is discussed in the section on mortise and tenon joints on pages 74–75).

Callipers, dividers and compasses

These tools are very useful in the workshop, but as they are most often used in the process of turning wood, they are discussed in more detail in that section (see page 95).

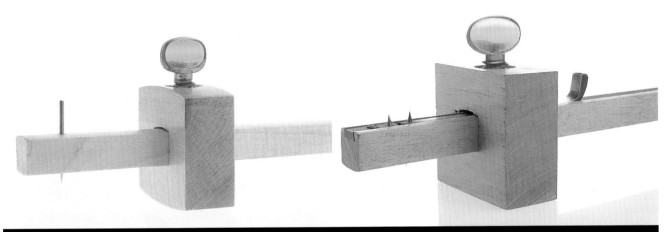

Marking gauge

Mortise gauge

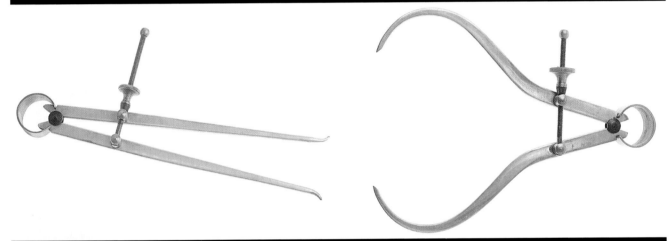

Internal calliper

External calliper

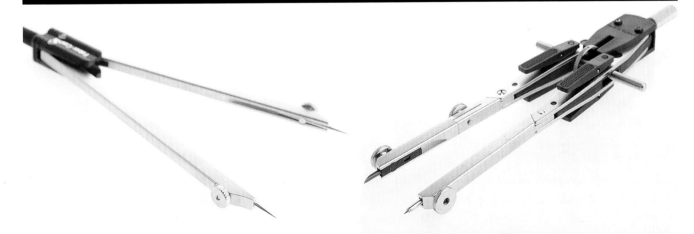

Dividers

Pair of compasses

You will need at least three of these tools for general use, and they are listed in order of necessity.

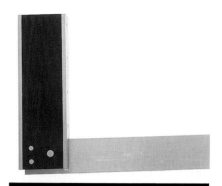

Try square

The two components of this tool are the blade, which is usually made of fine steel, and the stock, which is made either of wood or steel. The better-quality wooden stocks have a brass strip on the inside edge, which effectively gives greater accuracy and longer life. Some stocks have a 45° cut-away, which is useful for marking and checking 45° angles.

The try square has three primary uses: first, for drawing a square line across a piece of wood; second, for checking the squareness of the ends; and third, for testing the accuracy of joints that are being set.

Steel square

A steel square is much larger than a try square and has two blades, one being shorter than the other (about 400 mm/16 in and 600 mm/24 in respectively). One benefit over the try square is that all edges are marked in millimetres (or inches), which assists in marking out and checking work. Another difference is that the tool is flat and does not have a stock.

This square is mainly used for marking larger boards and for checking the accuracy of the corners of large jobs, such as book cases.

Combination square

A combination square features a 45° as well as a 90° angle. Some makes, such as the combination square pictured here, also have a spirit level and a blade, which is marked out in millimetres or inches, enabling it to be used in place of a steel rule.

Adjustable bevel (sliding T-bevel)

This tool has a blade that can be adjusted to almost any angle. It can be used as a square – although it is not as reliable in this use as a try square – or for marking 45° or any other angle. In this book it is used for marking out dovetail joints. The best method of setting this bevel accurately is to lay it on a plastic protractor and then set and fix it at the required angle. Because the blade protrudes from both sides of the stock, two angles are available and, as you may recall from your school geometry lessons, the two angles added together always add up to 180° (a straight line). For example, if the angle on one side is 45°, the other will be 135°.

The better-quality bevels have a brass or steel blade with a wooden stock, but the less expensive versions, with a steel blade and plastic stock,

Steel square

Combination square

Adjustable bevel (sliding T-bevel)

are usually quite adequate, particularly if not used that often. Some stocks have a slotted screw for fixing the blade in position, others have thumbscrews. The thumbscrew is easier to secure as you do not need a screwdriver, but because it protrudes from the stock it tends to get in the way. The choice is a matter of personal preference.

BASIC MEASURING AND MARKING TECHNIQUES

One of the most important aspects of a successful woodworking project is the accuracy of the measuring and marking out.

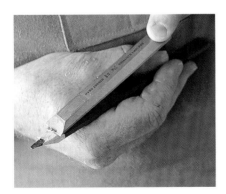

A carpenter's pencil with a rectangular point is stronger and better than an ordinary HB (no. 2) pencil, although both will do the job satisfactorily, as

long as the point is sharp. If the pencil is blunt, the mark made on the wood can be as much as 1.5 mm ($\frac{1}{16}$ in) wide, which can lead to errors when cutting.

When measuring, make sure that the tape or rule is held firmly on the surface of the timber before placing a single but clear pencil mark at the required length. Do not use a big round dot or thick line when marking out, as this again can lead to inaccuracy. When making the pencil mark, your eye should be directly above where the mark is being made. Drawing a small circle around the dot or an 'X' centring on the mark will help to identify exactly where it is.

When drawing a square line around a piece of wood, place the pencil point on the mark and slide the square up to the pencil, ensuring that the stock of the square is held tightly against the wood and that the blade is flat against the surface. Draw the pencil along the straight edge to form a clear line. You will notice from the photograph that the pencil is angled in towards the straight edge as this will ensure that the point is flush against the straight edge. When the line is established, measure the distance once again to check the accuracy before cutting.

Scoring the line with a knife blade or bradawl will make the line more visible, and will also prevent the grain being torn by the saw when you cut.

It is particularly important to purchase good-quality saws as these are the most frequently used tools in woodworking. The blade should be made from carefully selected steel and the handle from fine and carefully shaped wood or composite material, which is firmly secured to the blade. To test the quality of a crosscut or ripsaw blade, bend the tip right around to the handle and then release it. It should spring back with a good 'twang' and, as you look along the blade, it should be perfectly straight. Be careful when you do this – if you try this exercise on a cheap blade the shopkeeper may insist that you buy the saw, as he can no longer sell it with a right-angled bend in the blade!

A quality saw should ring like a bell and sustain the sound when struck with something hard. If you try this with a cheap blade, it will result in a dull 'thunk'. Buy saws that carry the name of a reputable manufacturer and you will never regret the additional cost.

Crosscut saw
This is the general workhorse of the woodworker's workshop and its primary use is for cutting across the grain of the wood.

The crosscut saw usually has about eight teeth per inch (25 mm), with each tooth sharpened like a knife and the teeth set alternately left and right. The sharpened tip of each tooth cuts the grain like a knife and the wood in the middle of the cut is pushed out as sawdust.

A panel saw looks very similar to a crosscut saw, but it is slightly shorter and the blade has more points per inch, allowing for a finer and smoother cut.

Ripsaw
The ripsaw is quite similar in appearance to the crosscut saw but, as its primary use is for cutting with the grain, the teeth have a chisel edge rather than a pointed edge.

This saw usually has five to six teeth per inch (25 mm) and, as with the crosscut saw, the teeth are set alternately left and right.

Tenon saw (back saw)
This is another general-purpose saw which, as its name suggests, is used for cutting tenons and for other cutting jobs that need a finer and more controllable saw than the crosscut or ripsaw. The tenon saw usually has

about 20 teeth per inch (25 mm) and a strong brass back, which gives stability and weight to the blade.

Dovetail saw
Essentially, this saw is a smaller version of the tenon saw and is used for very fine, straight cutting, such as for dovetail joints. Notice the different shape of the handle.

Coping saw
This saw has a fine-toothed, narrow but hard blade, and is used for cutting curves in thin wood (no thicker than 10 mm/ ⅜ in). The angle of the blade is adjustable so that the saw can be used to cut in any direction around the 360° of a circle.

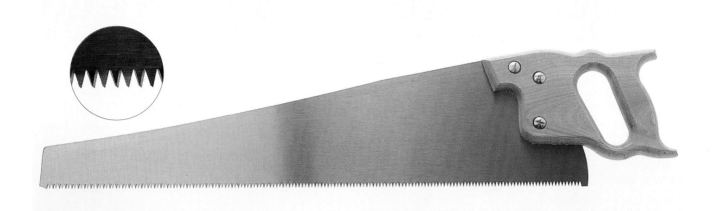

Crosscut saw

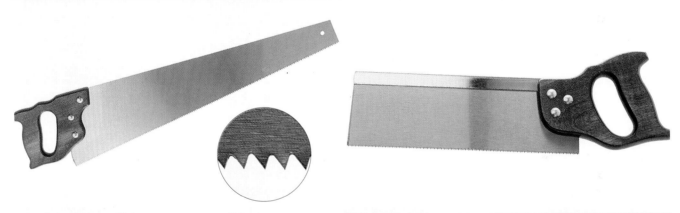

Ripsaw

Tenon saw (back saw)

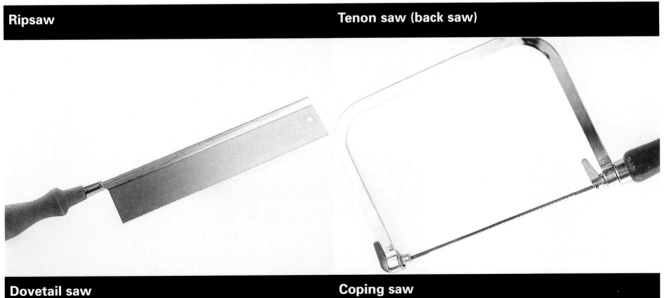

Dovetail saw

Coping saw

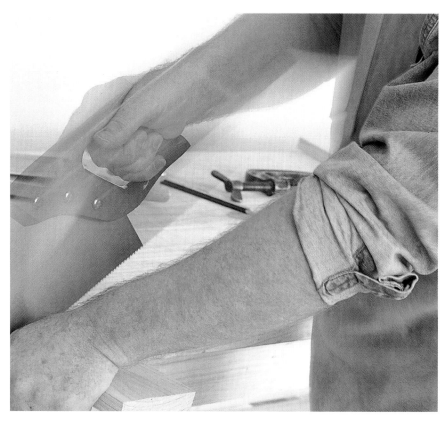

You will notice that the wood to be cut is firmly fixed to the work surface, the index finger of the hand holding the saw is extended for greater control of the blade, and all other fingers and thumbs are out of the way.

When using any hand saw, start the cut by gently drawing the blade backwards (the opposite way to the cutting direction) and making very short, light strokes until the cut is established.

After a few short strokes, gradually increase the length of the stroke until you are using the full length of the saw blade. Never force a saw to do its work – if the teeth are sharp, minimal downward pressure is required and the saw will work adequately. Also take long, slow strokes, as any attempt to saw quickly will probably result in inaccuracies, as well as the blade jamming in the cut.

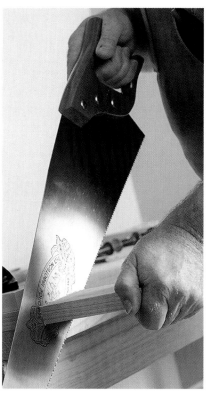

When nearing the end of a cut, ensure that the piece that is being cut off is well supported, as the weight of this surplus may pull down and cause the wood to split or tear before the cut is completed.

Planes are used for smoothing boards that have been sawn, for levelling off undulations and for finishing off prior to sanding, painting or sealing.

The photograph below shows the components of a metal bench plane, which will help you to understand how the plane works and will also be useful when you need to sharpen the blade (see pages 53–54).

Bench plane (smoothing plane)

Blade

Aligning lever

Cap iron

Lever cap

Front handle

Back handle

Adjusting wheel for setting blade depth

Face (underneath)

Jack plane

Block plane

Bench plane (smoothing plane)
A general-purpose bench plane is really the only tool in this category that the general woodworker will need. A model of about 260 mm (10¼ in) in length with a blade width of approximately 60 mm (2¼ in) should be sufficient.

Jack plane
If you want to add another plane to your collection, it is worth considering a jack plane (also known as a jointer plane). It is made of either metal or wood, is about 420 mm (16½ in) in length, and is useful for smoothing the

undulating edges of boards – the long foot rides over the undulations, allowing the blade to smooth off the tops.

Block plane
At the other end of the scale comes the short block plane, with a foot that is only about 120 mm (4¾ in) in length. It is particularly useful for cutting end grain and for getting into tight areas.

There are many other planes available, but these are usually of a specialized nature and can be difficult to obtain. Plough planes, rebate (rabbet) planes and shoulder planes have not been included in this section, as the work of these planes is now more easily accomplished with electric hand tools. It is worthwhile, however, to visit a comprehensive woodworking store and have a look at the planes available, not only for interest's sake, but also for the pleasure it would give you to own one or two of these specialized planes, even if you only use them occasionally.

BASIC PLANING TECHNIQUES

To set and adjust the depth of the plane's blade, turn it upside down and look along the face of the plane.

A few experimental turns on the adjusting wheel will allow you to see the blade extending or retracting from the face of the plane. It is important that the blade is parallel with the face and that only the tip is visible above the surface. Use the adjusting wheel to set the blade to the correct depth.

Make an experimental pass on the board to be planed to check whether the blade is set too deep or too shallow. The correct setting will result in a beautiful curl coming easily off the surface of the wood.

It is important to ensure that the entire face of the plane is in contact with the surface of

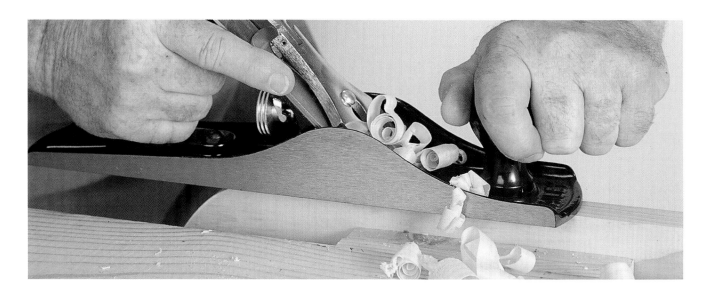

the wood, that the pressure from your hands is kept constant at the front and back of the plane, and that the position of your head is above and behind the plane, all of which will result in a good, balanced cut. You will notice from the photograph that the index finger of the driving hand is extended onto the side of the plane blade to help with directional control. The other hand is placed on the leading knob in such a way as to provide firm downward pressure at the same time as allowing directional control.

Always plane with the grain of the timber and not against it. Planing against the grain will jam the blade in the wood or will tear the shavings from the surface, leaving unattractive marks.

A few strokes across the face of the plane with a wax candle will assist tremendously in the smooth operation of the plane as it forms a light lubrication against the wood.

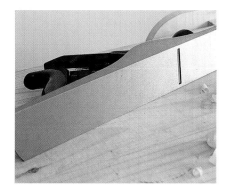

Always lay a plane on its side when it is not in use. If it is placed on its face this may damage the fine cutting edge, and cause marks on the planed surface when it is being used.

CUTTING AND SHAPING TOOLS: CHISELS AND GOUGES

The variety of chisels available is vast, but those listed here will form an adequate base for the general woodworker and will be applicable to most general uses. When selecting your set, there are a number of factors to be taken into consideration. First, it is important to select a tool made by a reputable manufacturer. The next consideration is the material from which the handle is made: chisels take a great deal of hammering (literally!), so a wooden handle, while feeling and looking better than a man-made composite, may shrink and split in the course of time. On the other hand, a composite handle doesn't look as good (especially if you're a traditionalist), but it is virtually indestructible. What it boils down to, however, is that the choice of handle is really a matter of personal preference.

A chisel should always be struck with a wooden mallet, and never with a hammer. Even if the handle is of a man-made material, the small striking area and sharp edges of a hammer can cause damage.

The width of the chisel's cutting edge is also important. Excluding the mortise chisel, three widths (6 mm/¼ in, 12 mm/½ in and 20 mm/¾ in) should be sufficient to start with, but if you want a fourth chisel, choose one with a wider cutting edge, for example, 25 mm (1 in).

Firmer chisel (framing chisel)

Bevel-edge chisels (paring chisels)

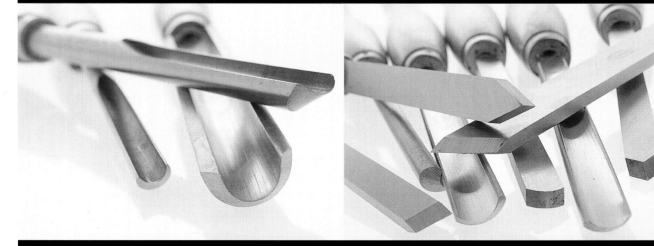

Gouges

Lathe chisels

Firmer chisel (framing chisel)

This is the most basic type of chisel. It has a flat, rectangular blade and can be used for a wide range of applications.

It has a few disadvantages, however, as it cannot be used effectively where an acute angle runs along the length of a cut (such as with a dovetail joint), but this drawback has been overcome in the more modern bevel-edge chisels.

Bevel-edge chisels (paring chisels)

Instead of being rectangular in section, the edges of this chisel's blade are bevelled (tapered) in towards the centre of the blade. This allows the cutting edge to get as close as possible to where it is needed in many applications.

Mortise chisel (not pictured)

This chisel is specifically designed for cutting the mortise section of a mortise and tenon joint. Because the cutting edge is usually narrow (about 6–8 mm/¼–⅜ in wide), the blade is thicker than most other chisels. This provides the necessary additional strength, as well as assisting in the accuracy of the cut.

The handle of a mortise chisel is more substantial than the other chisels mentioned above as it needs to withstand the continual blows of a wooden mallet when performing its main function.

Gouges

Gouges are chisels with curved blades (cutting edges) and are primarily used for cutting grooves and paring corners.

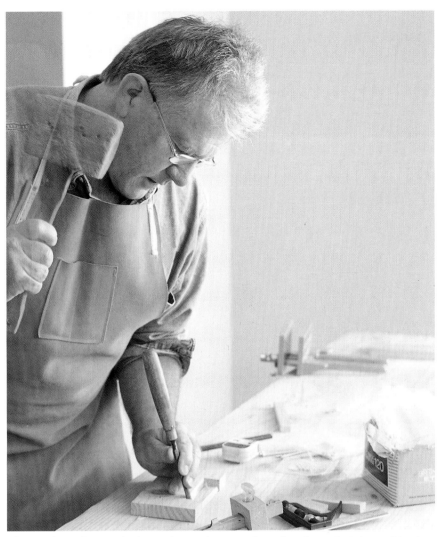

A good cutting technique depends upon keeping line of vision, chisel and mallet in alignment.

The cutting edge can be ground and sharpened on the inside of the curve for cutting grooves, or on the outside for paring. Although quite similar in appearance to lathe chisels, the handle of a gouge is shorter and thicker.

Lathe chisels

These tools are classified as chisels and look quite similar, but have an entirely different purpose to the chisels described above. They are used to 'peel' off wood while it is revolving on a lathe, and should never be used as conventional chisels. If the handles are struck with a mallet, they will shatter.

The blade is the same in cross-section as the firmer chisel, but there are many different shapes at the cutting end. The handles are usually made of wood and are longer than other chisels in order to provide better grip and leverage for lathe work. (For more detail on woodturning, see pages 92–97.)

SHAPING TOOLS

One of the joys of woodworking is the challenge of dealing with small and sharp curves and other oddly-shaped pieces of wood. In the modern workshop, many of these shaping jobs can easily be accomplished with an electric drill and an attachment. An electric tool, however, may not always be ideal for intricate jobs so, although the following five tools are not necessities in the workshop, it is worth your while adding them to your collection and learning to master the techniques of using them.

Spokeshave

As the name suggests, this tool was originally invented for shaping the wooden spokes of wagon wheels. It is essentially a very small plane designed for two-handed use. As with a conventional plane, the tool is pushed away from the woodworker.

The spokeshave can be purchased either with a flat bottom for working concave shapes, or with a rounded bottom for working convex shapes. If you decide to add a spokeshave to your tool chest, the flat-bottomed version is recommended.

Drawknife (not pictured)

It is rather unconventional to include this particular tool in a general woodworking book, but it is such a pleasure to own and use that I've included it with enjoyment rather than practicality in mind. The drawknife is an ancient tool and not at all easy to use. It consists of two handles with a single blade which, unlike

the spokeshave or the conventional plane, is drawn towards the woodworker. Although it is a very basic tool, it needs considerable practice and skill in order to master the technique, but the enjoyment of successfully using this tool makes up for all the difficulties and frustration in mastering it!

Although it may be difficult to track down, the drawknife can be purchased either with a curved blade, designed for hollowing out the seats of chairs and the like, or with a flat blade, designed for working the spokes of wheels and the shaped legs of chairs.

Surforms

It is not often that something new is added to the range of useful woodworking tools, but in recent years the Surform has been added to the repertoire of shaping tools.

The blades of these tools look quite similar to, and operate on the same principle as a cheese grater.

They are very useful for shaping concave curves, convex curves and inside work, although they leave a rough surface that needs careful finishing off. They are not all that easy to use as they tend to get stuck on the wood, and it is recommended that you put in quite a lot of practice on scrap wood before using them on a project.

Rasps and files

These tools are essential for the purpose of shaping wood, and they come in a great variety of shapes and sizes. They may be rectangular, half round, round, or triangular in section, with a variety of blades, ranging from a very coarse cut (for getting through work quickly) to a very fine cut (for finishing off).

The selection of rasps and files you choose will be a matter of personal preference – visit a comprehensive woodworking store to view their selection before making a final decision.

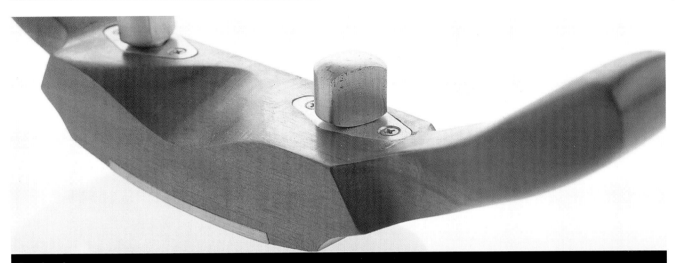

Spokeshave

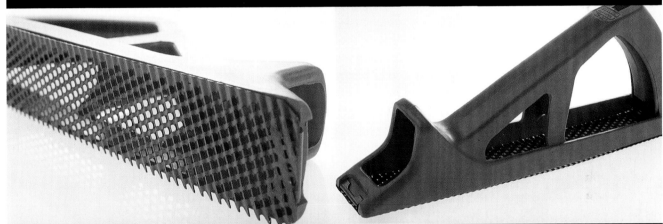

Surform blade   **Surform**

Rasps and files

BASIC SHAPING TECHNIQUES

Accurate shaping relies on having clearly marked lines on the wood, and the tool you use will depend upon whether the required shape is to be concave or convex.

When using hand tools, begin with a coarse tool, such as a Surform or rasp, and when the basic shape has been achieved, refine it with tools of a decreasing coarseness, finishing off with sandpaper.

Make sure that the wood is securely fastened to prevent any movement, and assess your progress with a visual inspection. Always file with the grain, as working against it will jam the tool or tear the wood.

DRILLS

In most woodworking jobs there is a need to drill holes into the wood to accommodate screws or dowels, or to assist in cutting out the mortise section of a mortise and tenon joint. Although most drill functions can be performed by hand-held electric drills or a drill press, it is good to own and be able to use a hand drill, as an electric drill can sometimes be too bulky to get into the available space. A hand drill is also far more effective during a power cut!

Wheel brace (hand drill)
The wheel brace is a very basic tool and is designed for light work, using a bit no larger than 5–6 mm (³⁄₁₆–¼ in) in diameter. This drill operates on a simple vertical crank drive and has an adjustable chuck that can accommodate a variety of drill bits. The thicker the diameter of the bit, the more difficult it becomes to turn the drill so, for holes greater in diameter than those mentioned, it is advisable to use a hand brace.

Wheel brace (hand drill)

Hand brace (chest brace or carpenter's brace)
This brace operates by turning a sweep handle horizontally. The leverage applied by this sweep is far greater than that of the crank handle in the wheel brace above, and therefore larger bits can be used. The adjustable chuck of this drill will accept much

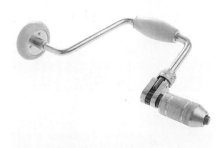

Hand brace (chest brace or carpenter's brace)

larger drill bits as well as auger bits specially designed for use with this tool. Substantial downward pressure can be applied by placing the flat handle at the top of the tool in the palm of your hand and then placing the back of your hand in the centre of your chest (hence the name). Most models have a ratchet so that where a full 360° sweep of the handle is not possible, the stroke can be reversed without turning the bit backwards.

DRILL BITS

Drill bits come in many shapes and sizes, but although they are designed for specific tasks, they all have basically the same function – to make a hole in a piece of wood, as cleanly as possible and to the exact size required. Each bit has a chisel-shaped cutting edge on either side of the centre of the bit, which cuts the wood and feeds it up the spiral clear of the hole.

Twist bits
These cylindrical bits are designed for use in a wheel brace or electric drill and for general woodwork ranging from 2–10 mm (¹⁄₁₆–³⁄₈ in) in diameter. The most common twist bit was originally designed for drilling metal, but is quite suitable for use with wood. The tip, however, may tend to 'drift' on the wood if not applied carefully, and may result in the hole not being exactly where you want it. Brad-point twist bits have a raised pin in the centre of the cutting surface, which leads the drill into the wood.

Flat bits (spade bits)
These are designed for use in a hand brace and are available in a variety of sizes. Their main use is for drilling holes of larger diameters, for example 20–30 mm (¾–1¼ in).

Auger bits
Use an auger bit that is designed for use with a hand brace for holes larger than 11 mm (⁷⁄₁₆ in) in diameter. This type of auger is not cylindrical and has a tapered rectangular end that fits into the chuck, giving far more leverage than the cylinder end of the conventional twist bit.

Adjustable bit
As the name suggests, this bit can be adjusted to the required size, saving you from buying a range of auger bits. The disadvantage, of course, is that every time you need to drill a different diameter, the cutting end has to be altered and then checked for accuracy.

Twist bits

Brad-point twist bits

Flat bits (spade bits)

Auger bits

Adjustable bit

Rose countersink bit

Depth stop

Countersink bits

Although these bits are not strictly used for drilling holes, they have been included here as an adjunct to the drilling process. The most common and useful of the many varieties available is the rose countersink bit.

A countersink bit is used to produce a conical shape to the lead hole for a screw so that the head of the screw will lie flush with the surface of the wood when it has been screwed into position.

Countersink holes can be drilled larger than the head of the screw so that it can be flush-filled with a suitable wood filler to cover the screw head and to match the surface of the surrounding wood.

Depth stops

Commercially produced depth stops are available in various sizes to fit most twist bits. They are very useful as they can be set to the exact required depth of the hole. This not only ensures accurate drilling, but goes a long way towards preventing a loss of temper, as there is nothing more frustrating than the drill bit 'erupting' on the other side of a piece of wood to destroy the look of an otherwise beautiful surface!

To save money, you can make your own depth stops. All you need to do is cut a small block of wood to the required length, then drill a hole through it to the same diameter as the bit you'll be using. You can also wrap coloured tape around the bit to indicate the correct depth.

BASIC DRILLING TECHNIQUES

There is a vast variety of drill bits, but the most important step before starting to drill is to select the correct bit for the job. For example, it would be pointless trying to drill wood with a masonry bit.

Whether using a hand drill or electric drill, ensure that the bit is firmly secured in the chuck and that the chuck is locked.

If the drill bit does not have a centre pin, use a nail punch to make a small indentation at the exact spot where drilling should commence. This will assist the bit to start exactly where you want it to.

Most holes must be drilled at 90° to the surface of the wood and it is helpful to keep your line of sight vertically above the drilling process. If you are not sure that you can rely on your visual judgement, place a try square alongside the job to ensure that the drill bit is placed as accurately as possible.

When drilling right through a piece of wood, place scrap wood underneath to stop the bit from breaking out on the far side and tearing the wood. For example, when using a flat bit, turn over the wood as soon as the centre tang penetrates, and drill again at that hole. This will ensure a clean cut from both sides. When withdrawing the drill, let the bit turn slowly in the same direction to release it cleanly from the hole.

Most woodworking jobs need glue to hold the joints and parts together and the glue needs time to set. This is where clamps and cramps come into their own as this is their primary function. These tools often need to be used in pairs, so owning two or more of each would be advisable.

G-clamps (C-clamps)
The shape of this tool gives it its name. In addition to being used to hold joints together until the glue has set, G-clamps are often used for securing wood firmly to the work surface so that no movement occurs when planing, cutting or sanding.

Each manufacturer has their own method of numbering the sizes of their clamps, so the sizes given below refer to the maximum stretch of the clamp. A good general-purpose size G-clamp is about 105 mm (4¼ in), but if you can afford it, purchase a larger pair of about 150 mm (6 in) as well as a smaller pair with a stretch of 70 mm (2¾ in).

G-clamp (C-clamp)

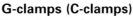

Sash cramp (bar clamp)

Quick-release clamp (speed clamp, F-clamp)

Sash cramps (bar clamps)

This cramp, based on a long, straight steel bar, has been developed for larger jobs. The end stop slides along the steel bar and can be set to the required length by the insertion of a steel pin into the appropriate hole in the bar.

The best method of using sash cramps is to put the pieces together before applying glue and then to set the end stop(s) of the cramp(s) to the correct length (insert pieces of scrap wood between the jaws to prevent bruising the project). The cramps will then be set and ready for use as soon as the job is glued and ready for clamping.

Quick-release clamps (speed clamps, F-clamps)

Although it looks similar in construction to the G-clamp, this clamp has a pump-action trigger that tightens the jaws with each squeeze. Because these clamps allow a greater variety of adjustment they are very useful and time-saving tools, but they are not essential.

of plywood to the same size as the ends of the clamp and glue them on with wood glue (top right). This makes them semi-permanent and has a distinct advantage as you often find that to hold the wood and the scrap and set the clamp at the same time requires at least two pairs of hands – a problem when working alone!

If there is any chance of glue seeping out of the joint onto the protective block of wood, place a piece of wax paper or greaseproof cooking paper between the protective block and the project (right). This will ensure that you do not end up with the protective blocks being firmly glued to your beautiful job!

Sometimes a sash cramp may not be long enough for the job in hand. A simple solution to this problem is to remove the end stops from two sash cramps and join them together using one of the pins and two G-clamps to prevent them coming apart.

For awkwardly shaped pieces, use a strap or cord and toggle system as an alternative to clamping (pictured below).

BASIC CLAMPING TECHNIQUES

When using clamps or cramps, it is advisable to place a piece of scrap wood between the steel jaws of the clamp and the wood on which you're working to prevent the wood being bruised by the pressure of the steel. Alternatively, cut pieces

Tools for gripping and pulling out old screws and nails are often needed, particularly when repairing or restoring furniture.

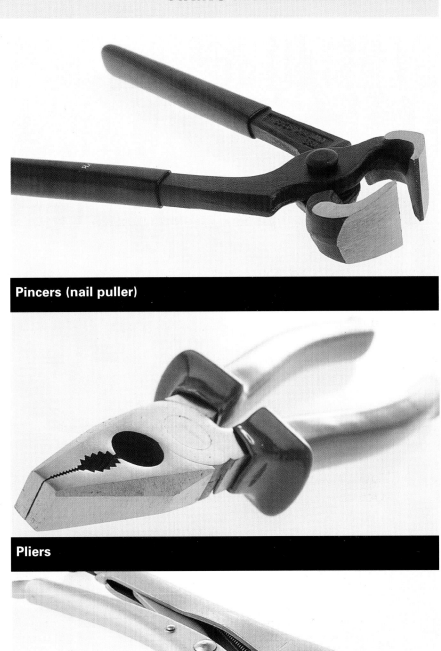

Pincers (nail puller)

Pincers (nail puller)
This tool is designed for extracting nails from wood. The face is curved so that it can be used in a lever action. It is advisable to place a bit of scrap between the tool and the wood on which you're working to prevent the metal of the tool from bruising the wood surface.

Pliers
Although not a woodworking tool, there are many occasions when pliers are useful for gripping, turning or snipping things. For example, a panel pin has the potential to split a thin piece of wood, wedging the grain apart, but snipping off the pointed end with a pair of pliers could prevent this from happening.

Pliers

Mole grips (locking pliers)
As with pliers, this is not strictly a woodworking tool, but mole grips are useful when something needs to be gripped very tightly. For example, when the head of a screw breaks off, mole grips can be used to grip the remaining screw shaft and then turn it out of the wood.

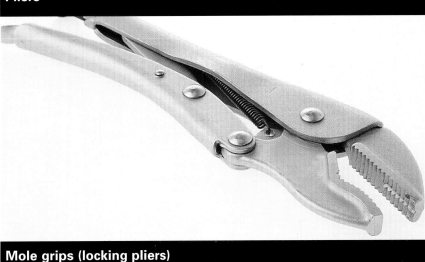

Mole grips (locking pliers)

Hammers are used for driving in nails, pins and wedges, for driving chisels when the chisel handles are made of a non-split, composite material, for drawing out nails and for knocking things apart. There are many styles of hammer heads and hammer handles available. Some handles are made of wood and leather, others of steel or composite plastic materials. The most satisfactory handles, however, are made of hickory or ash. The three hammers listed below should be adequate for the general woodworker's purposes.

Cross-pein hammer (Warrington hammer)

This general-purpose hammer is mainly used for knocking in nails and larger pins.

The pein (the tapered end) is used for starting smaller nails and pins that need to be held between the thumb and index finger. The tapered design enables you to drive in the pins without hitting your fingers, as can happen when using the broad, flat surface.

Pin hammer (tack hammer)

The pin hammer has the same design and is very similar in appearance to a cross-pein hammer, but it is lighter and has a slightly longer handle.

This hammer is designed for driving in panel pins, furniture tacks and the like, with the pein being a useful addition for starting small pins and tacks.

Claw hammer

This is heavier than the two previous hammers and often has a steel shaft overlaid with a rubber grip. Because the claw end is used for drawing out nails (as pictured on the opposite page), a wooden handle may not always be strong enough to cope with the leverage that needs to be applied.

Mallets

There are several different designs, but a carpenter's wooden mallet will be adequate for most of the general woodworker's or hobbyist's requirements.

The two main functions of this kind of mallet are for driving chisels when cutting and for gently knocking together joints. A mallet is usually made of beech and should be used in preference to hammers as the impact is less jarring. When knocking joints together with a mallet, the weight of the blow is spread over a much larger surface area compared to the relatively confined striking surface of a hammer. Therefore, if used properly, the mallet will not bruise or damage wood.

Cross-pein hammer (Warrington hammer)

Pin hammer (tack hammer)

Claw hammer   **Claw hammer extracting nail**   **Carpenter's wooden mallet**

SCREWDRIVERS

As screws come in a vast variety of shapes and sizes, the tools to turn them into place are specially designed to fit these sizes and shapes. Traditional wooden-handled screwdrivers are beautiful to look at and to use, but they are rapidly being replaced by screwdrivers with plastic or composite handles. There are, of course, many advantages to using these modern screwdrivers as they are usually less expensive, the handles are stronger and longer-lasting and there is virtually no chance of the blade working loose as it is moulded into the handle.

A basic range of at least three conventional, flat-bladed (8 mm/⅜ in, 4 mm/³⁄₁₆ in and 3 mm/⅛ in) screwdrivers should be adequate to deal with the variety of screws used in general woodworking, but you will need to add to your collection as the need arises – it is very important that the size of the blade matches the head of the screw. If the blade is too big, it will either not fit into the slot of the screw or the overhang of the blade will damage the wood as the screw is driven into place. If the blade is too small it tends to slip, damaging the slot until eventually there is no shoulder against which the blade can turn.

The screwdriver blade and screw head should be the same width.

Cabinet-maker's screwdriver

Primarily used by professional woodworkers, a typical example of this tool has a hardwood handle and a fine steel blade, but screwdrivers with plastic handles are also available. Most cabinet-makers prefer the feel of the shaped wooden handle as this allows the screwdriver to be used for a greater length of time without hurting their hands.

Ratchet screwdriver

Most woodwork jobs require the use of a number of screws, and one of the problems attached to this is the necessity of turning in all these screws, resulting in a sore wrist! To overcome this constant gripping and releasing of the screwdriver handle, some screwdrivers are manufactured with a ratchet, making it easier to turn and putting less strain on the wrist.

Spiral ratchet screwdriver (Yankee screwdriver)

The spiral ratchet screwdriver has a corkscrew action as the handle is pumped up and down. The thumb slide adjustment allows the direction or turn of the blade to be reversed or fixed so that this tool can be used both for screwing in and extracting screws, as well as making fine adjustments with a fixed blade. It also has a locking ring, which means that it can also be used as a conventional screwdriver.

A distinct advantage of this screwdriver is that it has a chuck that can incorporate a variety of blade sizes.

Multi-blade screwdriver

Essentially the advantage of this screwdriver is that it comes with a set of screwdriver blades that can be fitted into a chuck. If you would like to add one of these

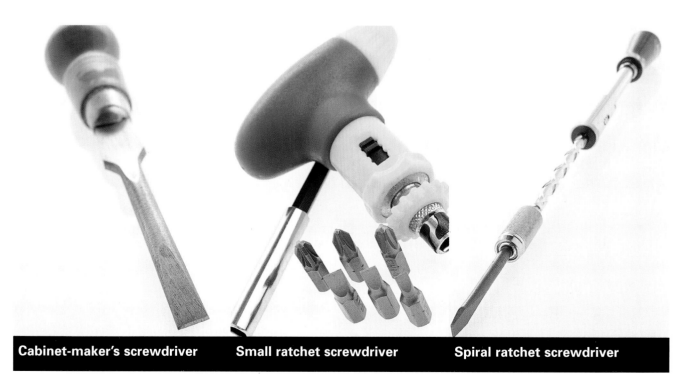

Cabinet-maker's screwdriver   **Small ratchet screwdriver**   **Spiral ratchet screwdriver**

to your tool set, be sure to buy a reputable brand as many of these tools seem to fall into the 'gimmick' category and therefore perform as a gimmick and not as a craftsman's reliable tool.

Cross-head screwdriver
The slotted-head screw has been used in woodworking for centuries, but in recent years the cross-head screw has become more popular (see the section on screws, nails and pins on pages 48–49). The essential difference between the two is that the cross-head screw head has an enclosed star rather than a single slot, and therefore requires a specially designed screwdriver to drive these screws home. Unless you have a multi-blade screwdriver, it is advisable to have at least two sizes of cross-head screwdrivers for general woodworking use.

SCREWS, NAILS AND PINS

The fixing devices that fall into this category are designed for specific purposes, and care should be taken to ensure that the appropriate fixing device is used for the application at hand. For example, it's very disheartening to come across a piece of furniture that has been 'repaired' by hammering a large nail through a dovetail joint in an endeavour to secure the joint again. A little thought, and the selection of the appropriate fixing device, will result in an excellent job.

Buying small quantities of screws, nails and pins in pre-packed bags is fine if you only need a few, but if you intend to work on a large job, this can be expensive. Ask for a whole box of screws, or buy nails and pins by weight.

Multi-blade screwdriver with flat and cross-head blades   **Cross-head screwdriver**

Screws

Screws come in many shapes, forms and sizes and are made of brass, steel or galvanized metal. The three main kinds of screw heads are the raised head, countersunk head and round head. Until fairly recent times, the screw head usually had a single slot, but the cross-head has become quite popular. It is sometimes called a star head and has a distinct advantage over the single slot in that it gives the screwdriver a more positive grip and results in less damage to the screw head if the screwdriver is not applied correctly.

It is a good idea to know how to order screws to avoid frustration for both yourself and the hardware store. Two measurements are used: the length and the thickness (gauge). The thickness is given as a number – the lower the number, the thinner the screw. For example, when asking for two dozen No. 8, 30 mm (1¼ in) steel countersunk head screws, 'No. 8' refers to the thickness of the screw and '30 mm (1¼ in)' refers to the length of the screw in millimetres (inches).

A chipboard screw has been developed in recent years to grip this notoriously difficult end grain. The screw is usually made of galvanized metal with a cross-head and a much wider thread than the more conventional screw. In effect, this means that it needs about half the number of turns to be screwed home, compared to the conventional screw. The shank of this screw is also narrower, which means that it is less likely to split the wood

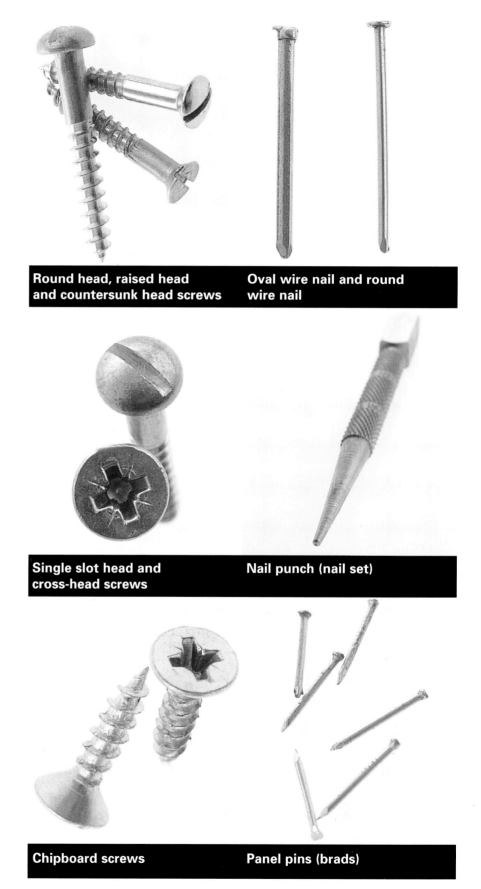

Round head, raised head and countersunk head screws

Oval wire nail and round wire nail

Single slot head and cross-head screws

Nail punch (nail set)

Chipboard screws

Panel pins (brads)

and requires a narrower lead hole. In fact, if you're working with fairly heavy timber and a powerful screwdriver, very often a lead hole is not required at all. This saves time, but great care needs to be exercised when using the screw this way, to ensure that the wood does not split.

Nails

The most common types of nails used in woodworking are the round wire nail and the oval wire nail.

Before you consider using nails instead of screws to secure pieces of wood, bear in mind the following three disadvantages. First, nails tend to split wood. If you decide to use nails, choose the oval wire nail over the round wire nail, as it is less likely to split the wood when driven with the head parallel to the wood grain. Second, because a nail secures wood by using friction (it bends the grain as it is driven home), it does not always make for a strong or permanent joint. Third, nails are much more difficult to remove once hammered home so, in the case of a repair or a mistake, part of the job may be severely bruised or even destroyed in an endeavour to remove the nail. It is advisable to avoid using nails in woodworking (at least the furniture-making aspects) wherever possible.

Panel pins (brads)

These are very small nails used for securing beading, moulding or panels. They come in a variety of lengths but, for the purposes of the general woodworker, a range of three lengths should be adequate (25 mm/1 in, 20 mm/¾ in and 15 mm/⅝ in).

The head of a panel pin is designed to be driven below the surface of the wood. The resulting small hole can then be filled with wood filler which, if properly applied and finished, leaves little evidence of the fact that a pin has been driven in at that point.

BASIC FIXING AND FASTENING TECHNIQUES

In nearly every kind of woodworking project, in particular furniture-making, it is preferable to make use of screws rather than nails.

A steel countersunk screw is the most practical screw for woodworking jobs, but the most important factor to remember is that you should always use a screw that is the appropriate size and type for the job you need to do.

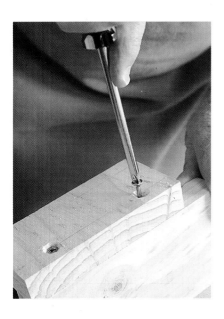

When joining pieces of wood of varying thickness, always screw through the thinner piece into the thicker piece as this will ensure a better grip for the thread of the screw.

When screwed in tight, the head of the screw should be 2–3 mm (¹⁄₁₆–⅛ in) below the surface of the wood. The resulting indentation can then be filled with matching wood filler to disguise the hole.

PILOT TOOLS

There are many occasions in woodworking when a pilot or lead hole needs to be used, either to prevent the tip of a drill bit from moving away from the intended spot of insertion, or to lead a screw point in the correct position or direction. Several tools have been designed for this purpose, but in this age of electric tools these hand-held pilot tools have largely become obsolete.

Gimlet

This tool has a long steel spike with a point resembling the tip of a screw. Above the tip is a cylindrical section similar to a drill bit, and this is topped by a wooden T-shaped handle. Although this tool is mainly used for making lead holes for screws, it can also be used to bore holes in wood, but this is a very laborious process.

Bradawl

There are several versions of this tool. A flat-bladed bradawl looks similar to a tiny screwdriver and is used by placing it on the required spot, with the blade lined up across the grain of the wood, where a simple twist of the wrist and some gentle pressure will drive it into the wood. A bradawl with a spiked tip not only has the advantage of being used for leading in a screw, but also for accurately marking centre spots. One disadvantage of the spiked blade is that care needs to be taken when applying this to the wood so that it does not 'drift'. The natural wood grain has both hard and soft areas, and the spike can drift away from the hard areas as the soft areas offer less resistance.

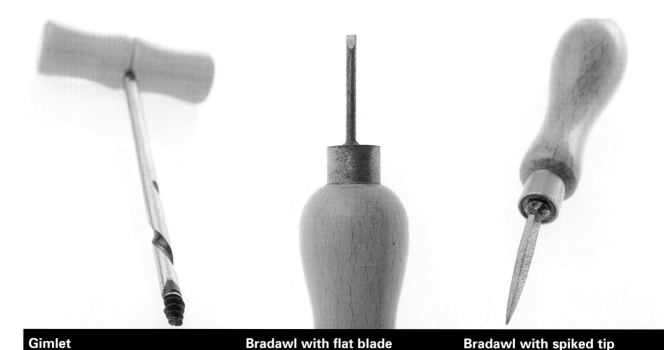

Gimlet   Bradawl with flat blade   Bradawl with spiked tip

After the wood or surface has been worked to the desired shape, it will be necessary to give the wood a fine, smooth finish prior to the application of sealing coats of varnish, oil or paint. In a modern workshop much of the finishing can be accomplished with the use of power tools, but there are usually some applications and corners that will need to be finished off by hand.

Cabinet scraper

The purpose of the cabinet scraper is to smooth the surface of a board and to remove any minor undulations and protruding grain. The most basic cabinet scraper is a rectangular piece of steel that is used in a two-handed fashion and is pushed away from the body.

There is another, more sophisticated and easier-to-use cabinet scraper, that is similar in appearance to a spokeshave, and accommodates the rectangular blade in a metal handle. The main difference between the spokeshave and cabinet scraper is the way in which the blades are sharpened. A spokeshave blade is sharpened in the same fashion as a plane blade, whereas a cabinet scraper blade has a square and 'burred' edge (see sharpening blades on page 54).

Hook scrapers (not pictured)

Another relatively modern innovation is the hook scraper (also known as a Skarsten scraper), a versatile and multi-purpose tool that can be effectively used instead of a cabinet scraper or, to some extent, a spokeshave. This tough little tool is also very useful for scraping paint and varnish off the surface of wood. The blades are replaceable, but considerable cost can be saved as these blades can be resharpened a number of times with a file or oilstone (see page 54).

Abrasive papers and cloths

The name sandpaper is still used as a descriptive generic term from the days when it was literally that; beach sand glued onto paper. Today's 'sandpapers', however, are much more sophisticated and use modern abrasives, such as silicone carbide and aluminum oxide, glued to either a paper or cloth backing. Generally speaking, the cloth-backed sandpaper is more durable than its paper counterpart, but it is usually more expensive.

Abrasive papers and cloths are commercially available in a variety of textures, from very

Cabinet scraper

Abrasive papers

Abrasive paper wrapped around a sanding block

coarse to very fine. A printed note on the back of each sheet usually gives a number followed by the word 'grit' – the lower the number the coarser the grit.

For the general woodworker three or four grades should be adequate. For example, use 80 grit for very coarse, 100 grit for medium, 400 grit for fine and down to 1 200 grit for a glass-like sheen.

Abrasive papers are very versatile and can be used with a sanding block for a large, flat surface, wrapped around the edge of a piece of scrap wood for smaller areas and corners, and wrapped around a dowel rod for sanding concave curves. Probably the most popular way of using abrasive papers is to fold the sheet about four times so that the paper forms its own pad.

SHARPENING BLADES

No matter how good the quality of steel blades, all of them will eventually go blunt with use. Working with a blunt blade can damage the wood and can be inaccurate, as well as difficult to use. It is therefore important that you check the blades' cutting edges frequently to make sure that they are sharp. Most blades are quite simple to sharpen and, as described below, can be sharpened by the general woodworker. Instructions for sharpening saw blades have been omitted as this tends to be quite tricky and is best left to a professional. Ask your local hardware store to recommend a good saw sharpener.

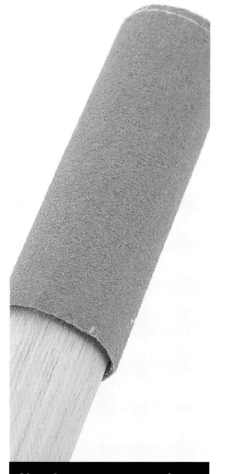

Abrasive paper wrapped around a dowel rod

Oilstones
This tool is absolutely essential when it comes to sharpening blades. Oilstones are available as both natural and man-made stones with varying coarseness. It is best to consult your local hardware store for advice on the most appropriate stone for your general woodworking purposes.

When sharpening a blade, first lubricate the stone with a light machine oil to facilitate the process. Move the blade in a figure-of-eight motion over the whole surface of the stone, otherwise the stone will become worn in the middle, causing it to become unusable.

Even if great care is exercised, it is inevitable that with constant use the surface of the oilstone will become pitted or concave. When this happens, find a flat piece of concrete paving, lubricate it with water and keep rubbing the face of the stone across the paving until a flat surface is re-established.

Sharpening chisels, planes and similar blades

Some care and practice is necessary to achieve a good cutting edge on chisel and plane blades. Two angles, about 30° for a grinding angle and between 35–45° for a cutting angle, should be adequate for general woodwork.

The grinding angle is best achieved using a slow-moving, water-lubricated, sandstone grinder, but most hobbyists do not have access to such luxuries. With a little practice the same result can be achieved using a coarse oilstone, a bench grindstone, or even a belt sander, provided that, in the case of the last two, the blade is handled very carefully and is kept cool by regularly dipping it in lubricating oil or a bowl of water. If the blade is not kept cool in this way, it will overheat, the edge will turn blue and the quality of the steel will deteriorate.

When the grinding edge has been established and the blade is square along its width, then the cutting angle can be

Oilstone

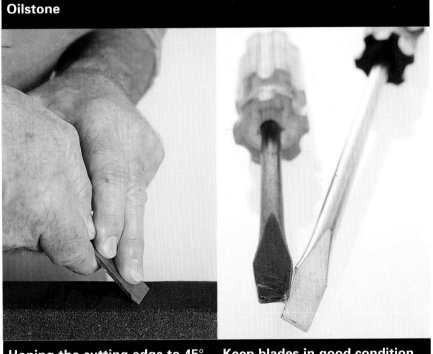

Honing the cutting edge to 45°   **Keep blades in good condition**

established. Gently apply the blades to the oilstone and, using a figure-of-eight motion, sharpen only the tip of the blade to 45°.

When the blade becomes blunt again with use, the cutting angle can be re-established quite easily, and

a number of times, without having to re-establish the grinding angle.

Once the cutting angle has been established, the flat side of the blade should be moved backwards and forwards on the stone to remove the burr. The final burr can then be

This photograph shows the complex design of a circular saw blade, which requires professional sharpening and balancing, without which there may be danger from vibration and jamming.

stropped away with a leather strop, leaving a very fine cutting edge. It should only be necessary to re-establish the grinding angle when the cutting edge has been re-established three or four times.

It is possible to buy a blade-sharpening guide into which blades can be clamped so that they can be sharpened to a perfect 45° angle. Your local hardware store will be able to assist you in choosing a suitable model.

Cabinet scraper blades

The primary difference between these blades and chisel and plane blades is that scraper blades are designed to scrape rather than cut. First,

form a grinding angle of 45° on a grindstone or oilstone, then establish a burr by securely fastening the blade in a bench vice, and drawing a hard steel shaft (such as a screwdriver shaft) across the blade.

Hook scraper blades

One of the benefits of the hook scraper is the facility to replace blunt blades with manufactured new ones. This can, however, be somewhat expensive if your scraper is in regular use, and it is therefore good to know that the cutting edge can be re-established several times before the blade is too worn to be of real use. Re-establishing the edge of the blade can be

achieved by securing the tool firmly in a bench vice and using a broad, fine file to sharpen the edge to the required angle.

Screwdriver blades

Screwdriver blades need to be sharpened when the blade becomes misshapen from excessive use. A good true edge can be established by using a grindstone or even a belt sander, if used very carefully. Only a tiny fraction of the blade should be removed in order to establish an edge that is square and true in all directions. The sharp corners of the blade can be removed to minimize potential damage to wood.

It should go without saying that tools (both hand tools and electric tools) and machinery are all potentially dangerous. This is particularly true of woodwork machinery, as evidenced by the fact that it is quite common to meet professional woodworkers who have fingers or parts of fingers missing, and sometimes even more serious injuries arising from accidents in the workshop. It is possible, however, to enjoy a long and productive woodworking hobby without losing the use of any parts of the human anatomy, as long as some basic safety precautions are adhered to. In particular, extreme care should be taken when using electrical tools and machines, as most of them have exceptionally sharp cutting blades or cutting edges that move at high speed.

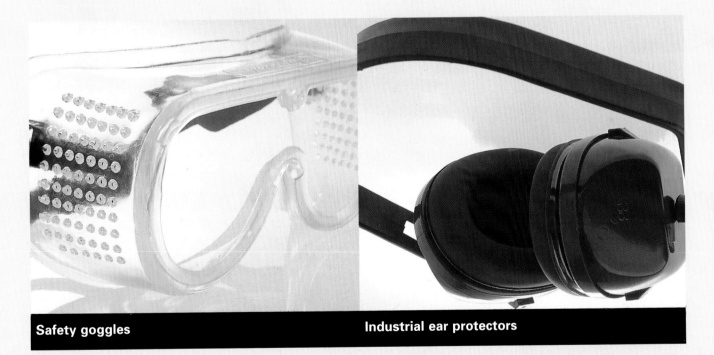

Safety goggles   **Industrial ear protectors**

▲▲ Always wear eye protection when using saws, lathes, electrical sanders or any other tool that is capable of throwing sawdust or chips around. Even if you wear eyeglasses to assist with your vision, it is advisable to wear protective goggles over these, as wood chips thrown out into your eye at high speed can, at the very least, be extremely uncomfortable and may cause permanent eye damage.

▲▲ Wear ear protectors when using electrical tools and machinery, as continued exposure to the noise can result in permanent injury to the very sensitive organs of the ear.

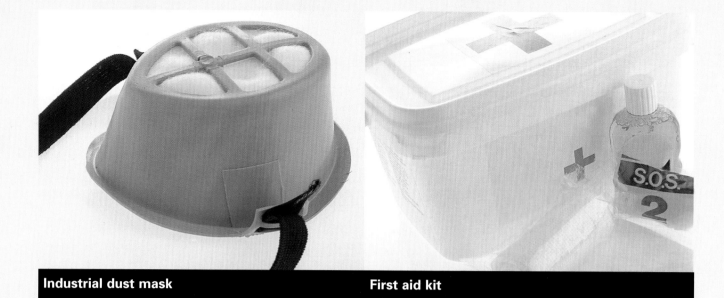

Industrial dust mask

First aid kit

▲▲ Sawing, planing and sanding create dust, particularly when working MDF (see page 16). Make sure that your workshop is well ventilated, and wear a dust mask to cover your nose and mouth.

▲▲ Always wear clothing that fits snugly as it is not uncommon for a loose sleeve or shirt tail to get caught in machinery, resulting in injury to the wearer (and damage to the machine). You should also remove jewellery and watches, tie back long hair, and remove ties and scarves.

▲▲ When using a crosscut or radial arm saw, keep your fingers and hands well clear of the blade. Only feed wood into the cutting area in the direction recommended by the manufacturer, and use 'push sticks' to finish the end of a cut through the blade. Make sure that the blade has a protective casing that leaves as little as possible of the blade exposed, and only move the cut wood away when the blade has come to a complete stop.

▲▲ Never make any adjustment to a machine without ensuring that it is switched off. In fact, as an extra precaution you should remove the plug from the wall socket.

▲▲ Always read and adhere to the tool manufacturer's safety instructions.

▲▲ Make sure that the tool's safety devices, such as blade guards, are in place and secure.

▲▲ Always think carefully about what you are going to do to ensure that the machine is capable of performing that task adequately and safely.

▲▲ Never force an electric tool or machine to do its work. In the case of a circular saw, this may cause the blade to jam or the wood to kick out. In the case of electrical sanders or planes, forcing the tool to do the job will adversely affect the surface of the wood, can cause injury and will possibly damage the machine or cause the motor to burn out.

▲▲ Make sure that your work surface is stable and solid.

▲▲ When working on an individual or small piece of wood, always ensure that it is firmly fixed or clamped to the work surface to prevent it from moving or slipping.

▲▲ Always have a first aid kit within easy reach to treat any minor injuries.

▲▲ Unfortunately, serious injuries do occur, so make sure that you are able to call somebody easily in the event of an accident. It is also advisable to let someone know how long you will be in your workshop so that they can check up on your safety if you take longer than expected.

HAND-HELD ELECTRIC TOOLS

There has never been a greater revolution in the history of woodworking than when machinery began to make its presence felt in workshops. The steam- and belt-driven machinery of the industrial revolution eventually gave way to electrically powered tools, which soon became economically viable and small enough to be used by the private woodworker as well as the furniture industry. Now, virtually every task in woodworking and furniture manufacture can be accomplished faster and more accurately by machine than by hand. However, a high degree of care and safety needs to be exercised when using any form of electrical tool or machinery.

Electric drills

The electric drill is probably the most versatile and ubiquitous tool in the workshop. Although its primary use is for drilling holes, the adjustable chuck can accommodate such a variety of attachments that it can be adapted to become a crosscut saw, jigsaw, sander or drill press, and can even be used to drive a small lathe.

Your choice of drill will depend upon the particular application you have in mind. Purchase a good quality model as the cheaper drills will not be able to stand up to much heavy-duty use.

Cordless drills

With the increase in the durability and power of batteries, the cordless electric drill has become very popular. This wonderful tool can be carried and used just about

Electric drill　　　　　**Cordless drill**

anywhere, as you are not restricted by the need for an electrical outlet and do not need to deal with the encumbrance of extension leads and cords. There are some disadvantages, however, as they are less powerful, slower and have a limited working time before the battery needs recharging.

Most models have speed control within the trigger mechanism and perform well as electric screwdrivers, particularly when the job requires many screws.

Drill bits for electric drills

If you look back to the section on hand drills and bits (see pages 38–40), you will notice that the bits listed there are also applicable to electric drills. However, because of the power and turning speed of an electric drill, other bits can be used for a variety of applications. These additional attachments make the electric drill an amazingly versatile tool. Hardware stores and woodworking tool specialists usually display as many as five or six different models together with the manufacturer's range of attachments and bits. For the woodworker it can be an enjoyable and enlightening experience to spend time comparing these products.

Router

The old English word rout means 'to force out', hence the name of this machine which 'takes out' wood in all kinds of applications. A router consists of an electric motor with a variable chuck on a large base

plate. In order to achieve a smooth cut and to prevent burning the wood, this machine turns at a much higher speed than any other electrical woodworking tool, which means that extreme caution must be exercised when using it.

The chuck firmly holds a cutting bit, and the face plate has a depth stop so that the cutter can be used in a variety of applications. Depending on the bit being used, the router is capable of cutting straight grooves through timber, dovetailing and cutting various shapes for mouldings and decorative edges.

The machine can be used in two ways, the most popular of which is holding the machine in both hands and applying the cutter to the wood, which is firmly fixed to the work surface. Alternatively, the router can be inverted and bolted to a commercial or home-built table, turning the machine into a spindle cutter. Using the router in this fashion means that the wood is applied to the fixed router, as opposed to the hand-held method, where the router is applied to the fixed wood. Extreme caution must be exercised when using this method as your fingers will be close to the cutting bit which revolves at a very high speed. Probably more fingers and fingertips have been lost in spindle cutters than just about any other piece of woodworking machinery.

Biscuit jointers

The biscuit jointer is a relative newcomer to the professional

woodworker's complement of tools but, although it is a very useful machine to acquire, it is not a necessity.

The machine is basically an angle grinder with a biscuit-jointing attachment that turns a small, broad blade (thicker than a circular saw blade) at high speed to cut a concave indentation into a surface that needs to be joined to another.

When a matching indentation (or slot) has been cut into each surface to be joined, a 'biscuit' is glued and inserted into the groove. A layer of glue is then applied to both surfaces and these are clamped together.

The inclusion of the biscuit makes for a much stronger joint than if the surfaces had simply been butt-jointed together. The biscuit is a more modern and much stronger alternative to using dowels in the same sort of application. You can see how this is used and applied on page 91.

HAND-HELD ELECTRIC SAWS

Circular saws

After you have bought an electric drill, the circular saw should probably be the next item on your list of tools to purchase. Blades for the circular saw are varied, enabling this tool to cut almost any material, from a very fine plywood to thick balks of timber, and from plastics to light metals.

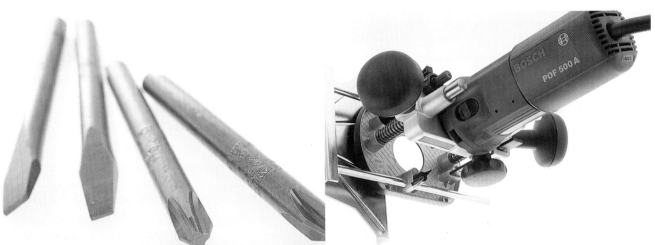

Screwdriver bits for use with an electric drill | **Router**

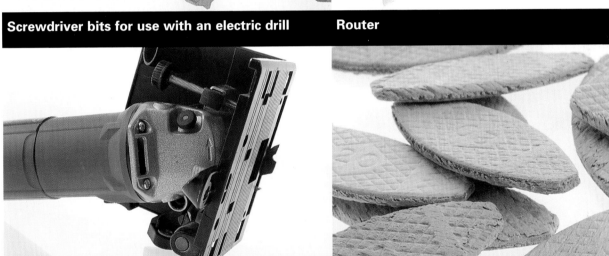

Biscuit jointer | **Compressed wooden biscuits**

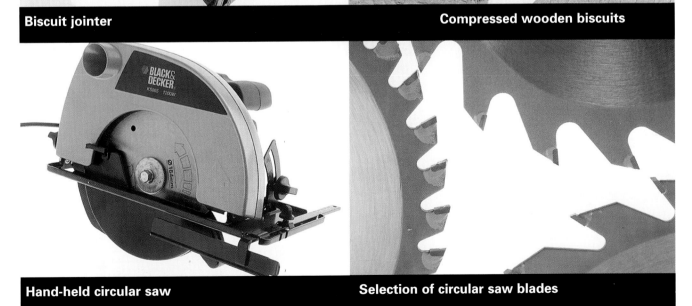

Hand-held circular saw | **Selection of circular saw blades**

The ripblade has coarse teeth designed for cutting with the grain down a length of timber.

The crosscut blade has smaller teeth than the ripblade and is designed for cutting across the grain.

Most manufacturers have designed a combination or general-purpose blade, which can be used either for ripping or crosscutting. This does go some way towards alleviating the necessity of constantly changing the blades.

Because a circular saw blade turns at high speed, extreme care needs to be exercised during its use. Think ahead: Is the wood firmly secured to the work surface?; Is the wood likely to splinter (this is particularly applicable when cutting plywood, which splinters and tears very easily)?; Is the blade likely to jam? See pages 55–56 for the safety precautions you need to take.

Most saws of this nature have a button to lock the trigger in the 'on' position, but I much prefer to keep my finger on the trigger – a saw running around the workshop on its own is not a situation worth contemplating!

Hand-held jigsaw   **Selection of jigsaw blades**

Hand-held electric plane

Hand-held jigsaw

The cutting action of a jigsaw is a vertical up-and-down motion. The teeth of a thin blade cut the wood on the upward motion, thus holding the wood firmly against the base plate. This saw is particularly useful for cutting around curves.

As with any other electrical or machine saw, various blades are available and the selection depends upon the thickness and type of wood that needs to be cut. Your hardware store can advise you of the type of blade needed for each application.

It is a good idea to keep three or four different types of blade in your workshop – also keep some spares because jigsaw blades tend to break quite easily.

Jigsaws come in a variety of makes and may have extras such as blade speed control built into the trigger mechanism, or a device that turns the blade, making it a multi-directional cutting device. A circle-cutting guide can be purchased as an attachment and will enable you to cut perfect circles. Most jigsaws also come with an adjustable base plate so that the angle of the blade can be adjusted to cut bevels.

Hand-held electric planes

These tools are particularly useful for smoothing the surface of rough-sawn timber prior to setting face sides and face edges. Each manufacturer has their own particular design specialties built into the machine, as various widths of cut are available. A blade width of 70–80 mm (2¾–3⅛ in) should be adequate for the general woodworker.

Electric planes also have adjustable depth settings so that they can be used for removing substantial quantities of wood or for preparing surfaces with a fine cut prior to finishing.

They work well when cutting with the grain, and it is recommended that they never be used to cut across the grain of the wood as this is likely to chip or damage the surface.

When planing with the grain the plane should be moved fairly slowly, otherwise a series of parallel grooves, which are difficult to remove, will be left on the surface of the wood. If you are using an electric plane for the first time, it is advisable to put in some practice on scrap wood before using the plane on a proper job.

HAND-HELD ELECTRIC SANDERS

These machines and attachments are a real boon when it comes to finishing off a job prior to sealing or varnishing, as they minimize an enormous amount of repetitive, dreary and wrist-aching work.

Disc sanding attachments

These attachments for an electric drill are available in a variety of styles, from slim rubber pads with a fixed shaft to thick and relatively cumbersome pads with flexible shafts. The flexible shaft enables the pad to maintain full surface contact with the wood, regardless of the angle of the drill.

The sanding discs themselves are also available in the same variety as described in the section on abrasive papers and cloths, so that the disc sander can be used for just about anything, from 'ripping' paint off wood to producing a very fine and smooth finish. However, care must be taken when using a disc sander as there is a tendency for the abrasive disc to leave score marks on the surface, particularly across the grain, if too much downward pressure is applied.

The abrasive discs for use on this tool can be purchased ready-made or, as an economic alternative, you can purchase standard sheets of abrasive paper and cut the discs yourself. Some discs are manufactured with a Velcro-type backing, which sticks onto the pad. This is very useful when it comes to changing the abrasive disc. This does mean, however, that you will have to purchase the ready-made discs rather than being able to cut them out yourself.

Flap sanding attachments

These sanding attachments (also for use with an electric drill) are made up of a central cylinder with a large number of abrasive paper or cloth flaps secured to it. Flap sanders are very useful for cleaning wood and particularly for getting into concave spaces or shapes. They can be purchased in various sizes, shapes and degrees of coarseness, and a trip to your hardware store will help to decide which type you need for the particular application you have in mind.

Belt sanders

This type of sander has an electric motor that pulls a continuous belt of abrasive material across a fixed face plate. It should be used only to sand with the grain, otherwise unsightly scratches will occur. These are very difficult to remove. The machines come in a variety of belt widths and lengths, but a belt width of 70–80 mm (2¾–3⅛ in) will be adequate for the general woodworker. The abrasive belts used in this machine vary from very coarse to very fine abrasive paper for finishing off.

Orbital sanders

The orbital sander has an abrasive paper or cloth fixed to a flat base plate and is driven by an electric motor that causes the base plate to vibrate (as with a Delta sander) or move in small circles at high speed. This is a great tool for finishing off all kinds of wooden surfaces, but care must be taken to apply very little downward pressure on the machine. Allow the weight of the machine to do the work otherwise the surface will be scored with small, grooves that are difficult to remove.

The abrasive sheets for all types of orbital sanders can be purchased ready-made or you can cut them to size from standard sheets of abrasive paper or cloth. A superb final finish can be achieved when a very fine abrasive material is used with this machine.

MACHINERY

Radial arm saw

This rather unusual looking machine is mainly used to rip or crosscut wood.

When using the saw for crosscutting, the wood is held against a guide and the blade, which is attached to the motor on the overhead arm, is drawn across the timber.

When ripping wood, the blade on the overhead arm is swivelled through 90° and the wood is pushed through the blade by hand (use a 'push stick' when nearing the end of the timber length so that your fingers and hands are well clear of the blade). You should always stand to the side of the machine and not behind the wood you're pushing through, as the blade can jam, causing the wood to 'kick back' out of the machine at high speed. Needless to say, this could result in a serious injury.

The radial arm saw can also accommodate a number of other attachments. These replace the cutting blade and convert the saw into a router or spindle cutter. Because the blade in both of these applications is exposed and spinning at high speed, extreme care must be taken to adhere to the manufacturers' safety instructions.

The physical size of the motor may result in the machine being slightly under-powered for applications such as ripping. In this instance, the wood may need to be passed through the machine a number of times, setting the blade a little deeper at each pass. This can be time-consuming and frustrating work, but the versatility of the machine makes up for this.

Several styles of cutting blade are available for the radial arm saw, but two blades should be sufficient for the general woodworker and hobbyist: a general-purpose blade, which is a combination rip/crosscut blade, should be adequate for most purposes; and a blade with very fine teeth can be used for very fine cutting, such as thin plywood.

Always disconnect the saw from the electrical power source before changing blades.

Table saw

As the name implies, this saw is fixed to the underside of a

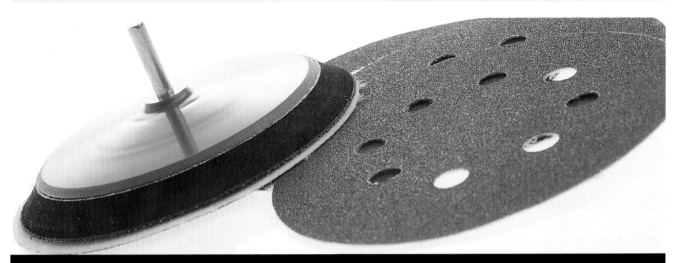

Disc sanding attachment

Flap sanding attachment   **Hand-held belt sander**

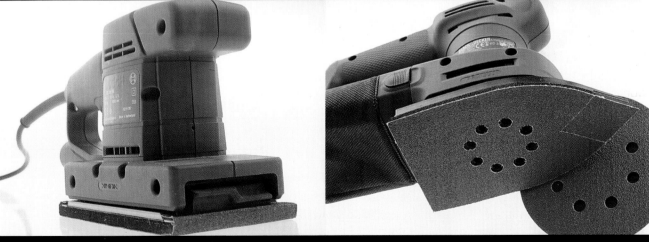

Hand-held orbital sander   **Hand-held vibrating orbital sander (Delta sander)**

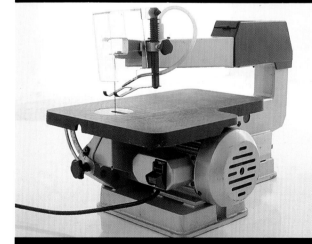

Radial arm saw

Table saw

Jigsaw (scroll saw, fret saw)

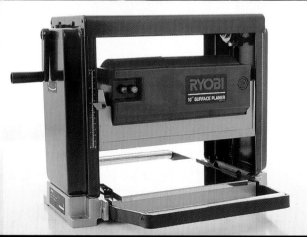

Planer-thicknesser

steel table. It is usually a much more substantial saw than the radial arm saw as it has a more powerful motor. This means that it will rip down a board of timber in one cut, instead of taking two or three passes as you would need to do with a radial arm saw.

There are, however, some disadvantages to this type of saw. Because the cut is made from the underside of the wood it is difficult to see where you are cutting, whereas with the radial arm saw the cut is made on the visible surface of the wood. Another disadvantage of the table saw over the radial arm saw is that it is considerably more difficult to remove and change the blade.

The choice between whether to buy a radial arm saw or a table saw is largely a matter of personal preference but, money permitting, it is useful to have one of each. The table saw can then be used for heavy-duty work, while the radial arm saw can be utilized for lighter work and more accurate cutting.

Band saw (not pictured)
The blade of the band saw is a continuous belt and is usually very narrow.

Band saws are available in two forms, a table or bench-top version with three wheels, or a larger, freestanding model on two large wheels.

This saw can be used for cutting gentle curves as well as straight lines and will accomplish much of the work of a tenon saw, and in a fraction of the time! Although the blade in all makes and models is fixed, the table is

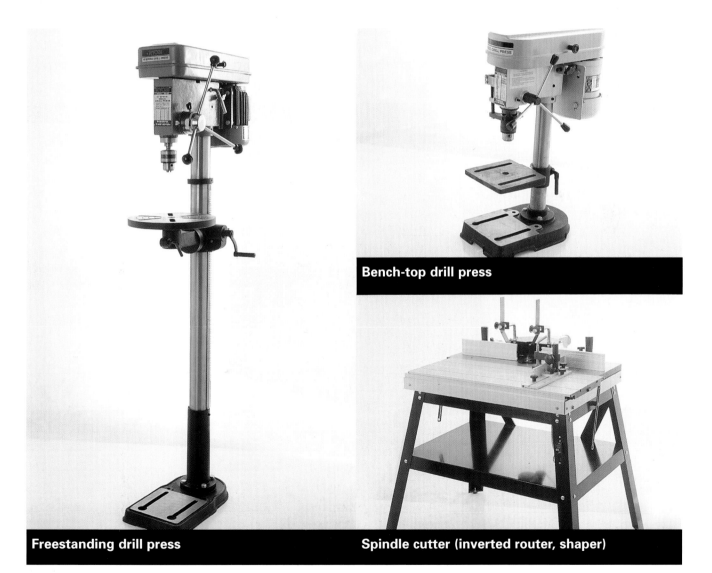

Freestanding drill press

Bench-top drill press

Spindle cutter (inverted router, shaper)

usually adjustable, making the band saw suitable for cutting mitres as well as 90° angles.

Jigsaw (scroll saw or fret saw)

This type of saw is used for cutting tight curves in wood that is no thicker than about 10 mm (⅜ in). The hard steel blade is very thin and has very fine teeth. It cuts in a vertical motion at high speed.

Planer-thicknesser

This is a wonderful machine to have in your workshop if it is within your financial means. Apart from general planing work, the planer-thicknesser will enable you to plane rough-sawn wood to perfection. If the machine has a thicknessing facility, another advantage is that when you need wood of an unusual thickness you will be able to plane down the wood to your exact specifications without needing to ask the woodyard to do it.

Belt sanders

This is a larger and fixed version of the hand-held belt sander and has the distinct advantage that, as well as being used for general flat sanding work, it can also be used very accurately for shaping wood, as both hands remain free to hold and manipulate the timber.

For the purposes of the general woodworker, these machines are best purchased as freestanding versions, as they are not used all that frequently and are small enough to be stored and moved quite easily.

Drill press

The choice of a freestanding or bench-top model depends largely upon personal choice and available budget, although it's as well to remember that the bench top version is usually very heavy and will have to remain in one place.

Because the table can be set at exactly 90° to the drill bit, it is a very accurate machine to use, not only for drilling holes, but for drilling out such things as mortise slots.

With most of these machines the drill chuck and shaft is connected to the motor by a rubber belt that can be shifted to smaller or larger wheels, therefore decreasing or increasing the speed of the bit. Often the highest speed setting enables you to use the machine as a router, but be careful when using it this way as the blade will be exposed.

Spindle cutter (inverted router, shaper)

A commercially manufactured spindle cutter is usually a very large, heavy and expensive piece of equipment. It is possible, however, to buy a table with an insertion plate to which a hand-held electric router can be bolted, turning the router into a spindle cutter.

If finances permit, it is ideal to own two routers, one of which is permanently attached to the table for use as a spindle cutter, and the other which is freestanding for ordinary routing work.

A wooden strip can be clamped onto the work surface to act as a guide for the wood being run across the blade.

THE MOST IMPORTANT TOOLS

There will be as many opinions on this subject as there are woodworkers, but the following list serves as a suggestion of the tools you will need, according to priority.

This basic set will help you get started and is useful for dropping hints for birthday and Christmas gifts!

- Tenon saw (back saw)
- Retractable steel tape measure
- 10 mm (⅜in) and 25 mm (1 in) bevel-edge chisels (paring chisels)
- Carpenter's wooden mallet
- Two 105 mm (4¼ in) G-clamps (C-clamps)
- Try square
- Cross-pein hammer (Warrington hammer)
- Bench plane
- Wheel brace (hand drill), or preferably an electric drill
- Set of drill bits (preferably brad-point twist bits)
- Two different sized flat-bladed screwdrivers and two cross-head screwdrivers
- Abrasive papers

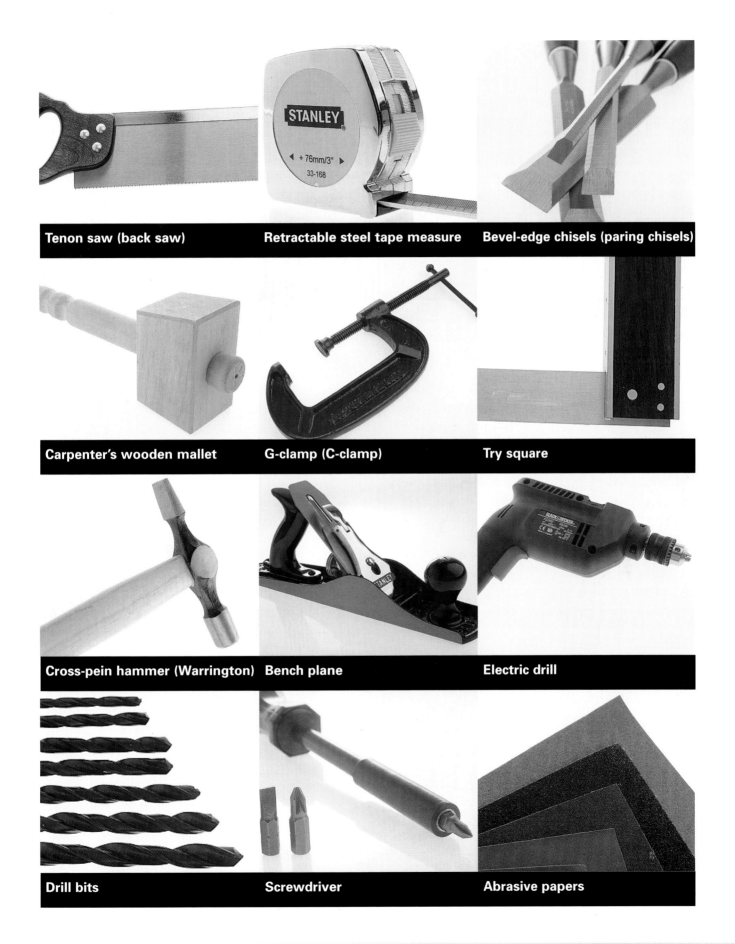

Tenon saw (back saw)

Retractable steel tape measure

Bevel-edge chisels (paring chisels)

Carpenter's wooden mallet

G-clamp (C-clamp)

Try square

Cross-pein hammer (Warrington)

Bench plane

Electric drill

Drill bits

Screwdriver

Abrasive papers

joining wood and turning

In most woodworking projects, separate pieces of wood have to be joined together in order to create a structure. Over the centuries many methods of joining wood have been invented and then refined or rejected, until today we have a relatively small collection of commonly used joints that can be adapted to almost any job.

Of course, one of the major advantages that technology has given us in this area is the superior quality of modern wood-joining glues. Before glues had been invented, the joints alone had to provide the fixing and the strength. An example of this can be found in the old 'refectory' style furniture, where a stretcher would be mortised through the shaped legs and then secured in place with a wedge. This wedge not only held the ends together, but also gave strength to the structure.

As we describe, illustrate and teach you how to make some of the most useful and popular joints, we suggest that you practise making a few of these before trying them out on an actual project.

This exercise has a number of distinct advantages. It will give you the opportunity to 'get the feel' of the tools used, while at the same time honing your woodworking skills. It will also save money and the excruciating frustration of cutting a joint incorrectly, resulting in the demise of your entire project.

The more you practice, and the more experience you accumulate, the easier the task becomes and the better the results.

PREPARATION

Many excellent books have been written about woodworking and, like every other subject requiring any level of learning and skill, the more you read and learn, the better. Read books on woods, tools and techniques and purchase a few reliable reference works that will improve your knowledge and skill. The following few introductory hints and comments will give you a good start, but you should never stop learning and improving!

RULES THAT SHOULD NEVER BE BROKEN

Never rush a job

Working with wood and making furniture is a most enjoyable hobby, but it is good to remember that the faster you try to complete a project, the more mistakes you are likely to make – and this even applies to the most professional woodworkers.

To avoid making these unnecessary mistakes you will need to plan your projects well in advance, and you will also need to plan carefully.

If you try working to a tight deadline, you are likely to make basic errors that will eventually cost you time and money. Take your time when measuring, cutting and finishing off.

Enjoy the time you spend in your workshop, and you will gain an enormous amount of fulfilment and satisfaction from it.

Measure twice, cut once

It's not difficult to rectify a mistake when measuring for a cut, but when you have already cut to a wrong measurement and find that your lovely piece of wood is the wrong size, the waste and frustration involved can be very upsetting.

One way to prevent this from happening is to take your measurement and make a small pencil mark at the correct spot. Take your tape measure away, check that you have read the measurement on the plan correctly and then measure the same piece again, if possible from another direction. If the two measurements and plan are the same, then it should be safe to make the cut.

If you follow this simple but logical rule, frustration will be kept to a minimum.

MARKING FACE SIDES AND EDGES

Most of the wood you buy for making projects will be almost ready to work. In other words, all the surfaces should be clean and flat, the corners should be square and the sides or edges will be square to the surfaces. However, this is not always as accurate as it should be, and some pieces may need further preparation before they are ready to use. In this case, do the following:

Use a try square blade to check that the face side is flat and true.

Establishing the face side

This is the surface that will be visible in most jobs. Choose the best-looking surface and make sure that it is flat and smooth by checking it with a steel rule or square. If the surface needs to be smoothed, a bench plane or hand-held electric plane is the best tool to use. When you are satisfied that the surface is flat in every direction, choose the side that is going to be the face side and place your face side mark against that edge.

Establishing the face edge

Having selected your face edge, two considerations are important for getting this edge true. First, the face edge needs to be as smooth as possible. This can be checked with a steel rule or square as was done for the face side. Second, the face side must be as square as possible to the face edge. The surface may need to be planed to achieve this and must be checked regularly with a square to make sure that the

face side is true and square to the face edge. When you are certain that this is accurate, pencil on the face edge mark.

If the face side has undulations and is not completely flat and true in all aspects, and if the face edge is not exactly square to the face side, inaccuracies can occur throughout the rest of the job, so it's worth investing a bit of time getting this right.

Face side mark

Once you have prepared the piece of wood and the face side is flat and level, draw a face side mark on the surface touching the edge, as can be seen in the photograph below.

Face edge mark

When the face edge has been established, draw a face edge mark (an inverted letter 'V') on the face edge, which touches the face side mark (see the photograph below).

Every piece of wood with which you work should be marked out in this way. The face side is the first to be established, followed by the face edge, and if these two edges are correctly and accurately prepared, all other measurements for width, thickness and length can be taken from these two surfaces.

The accuracy of the entire project will rely on these first and most important steps, and it is worth taking your time to ensure that it is done properly.

Establishing the correct thickness

If you are unable to buy timber in the exact thickness you require, there are several options open to you. You can ask the timberyard to put it through a planer-thicknesser to establish the correct thickness; you can use your own planer-thicknesser to achieve this; or you can do the following:

First pencil in the face side mark and then the face edge mark when these two surfaces are flat and square to each other.

Make sure that the face of the marking gauge is held flat against the face side.

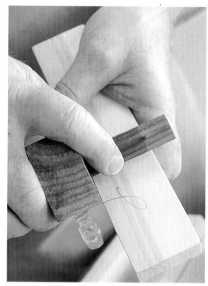

The pin of the marking gauge should be angled away from the line being marked.

Hold the blade and stock of the try square firmly against the wood to establish accurate square lines.

Set a marking gauge to the required thickness and, working from the face side only, establish a line all the way around the wood. Run a sharp pencil point along the line to make it more visible.

Keep checking your progress as you plane down to the marked line.

Fix the wood (face-side down) in a bench vice to prevent it sliding off the bench, and plane the surface down to the marked line. Use a steel rule or try square to check that the surface is flat and true.

Establishing the correct width

This is achieved by using the same method for establishing the thickness, except that the marking gauge is set against the face edge. Fill in the indentation left by the marking gauge with a sharp pencil, secure the wood in a bench vice and plane it down to the marked line. Use a square to check that all edges are square (at 90°) to each other.

When you are satisfied that the piece of wood is the correct width and thickness, the next stage will be to get it to the correct length. To do this, you must first establish one square end.

Establishing one square end

Lay a square as close to the chosen end as possible, making sure that the stock of the square is firmly against the face edge, and draw a line across the face side.

Make sure that the pencil point is sharp, and angle it in towards the blade of the square so that the line is drawn as close as possible to the edge.

The square line must be extended onto all four surfaces to accurately establish one square end.

When this line is accurate on the face side, reverse the square and draw a pencil line down the face edge and the opposite edge.

Cutting the end square

The line you make on a piece of wood indicates the exact position of the cut you want to make. Therefore always cut or chisel on the scrap side of the wood (the side you want to remove). If you cut on the line you will be cutting into the measured part, and the end result will be inaccurate.

Make sure that the saw blade is held square, both horizontally and vertically, to the marked line.

One method to ensure that the cut is accurate is to chisel a groove into the cutting line on the scrap side of the wood. This will help to keep the saw exactly to the line as you are cutting away at the scrap. When you have completed the cut, check that the end is square and true in all directions.

Establishing the correct length

Now that you have one square end, it is a relatively simple procedure to measure from this square end and mark the required length (remember, measure twice, cut once).

When you are sure that the measurement is correct, use your square to draw square lines all the way around the wood at the correct length, in the same way as for establishing the square end.

When this is done, score or chisel the line and cut away the scrap. You should now have a piece of wood that is exactly the correct width, thickness and length, as well as being square and true in all aspects.

A WORD ABOUT GLUE

White wood glue   **Epoxy glue**

Probably the most satisfactory wood glue available on the market for furniture-making is white PVA (water-based) glue.

This glue, however, is not impervious to water and is therefore not suitable for use on wood that is to be placed outdoors (the joints will weaken and could fall apart if exposed to damp or wet conditions). Use a good-quality, water-resistant glue for outdoor furniture – your local woodwork store can advise you as to which is the most suitable.

Epoxy glues come in two containers or tubes and must be mixed together in equal amounts. They are transparent and waterproof, and because they dry very quickly, must be used as soon as they are mixed.

Although epoxy will do the job, especially for repairing joints as they dry hard, even in gaps (which white PVA doesn't do), they are much more expensive than white PVA glues and are more difficult to use.

Contact adhesives are not suitable for joining wood.

Joints for flat rails and corners

MORTISE AND TENON

This is one of the joints that has 'stood the test of time' and has been used for hundreds of years in the construction of tables, chairs and stools. If you examine these pieces of furniture, you will notice that the mortise and tenon can be used for top joints or for joints within the leg or rail.

The mortise and tenon joint is very strong because the strength of the wood is not compromised as, although one-third is taken from the mortise section and two-thirds from the tenon, the combined original strength of the two is restored when they are glued together.

1 Establish exactly where the joint is to be made, and use the try square to draw square lines right around the wood.

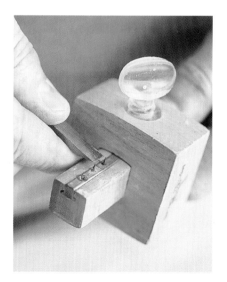

2 Set the two pins of the mortise gauge at exactly one-third and two-thirds of the width of the wood.

3 Working from the face side on both pieces, mark the guide lines for the mortise hole and the tenon cut. Draw in these lines with a pencil point.

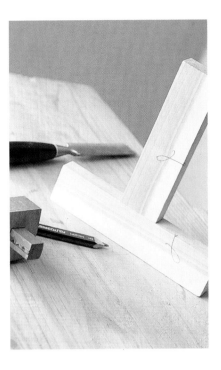

4 A drill press is useful at this stage to drill out the bulk of the mortise hole. Use a drill bit about a millimetre (¹⁄₃₂ in) narrower than the hole should be. If you do not have access to a drill press, fix the wood firmly in a bench vice and drill out the hole with a hand-held electric drill, making every effort to ensure that the drill is vertical to the wood.

6 Now on to the tenon section. Use a tenon saw to cut down the wood on the scrap side of the tenon lines so that you have a completed tenon, which looks like the one in step 7 below.

8 When the joint fits well, apply glue to all the surfaces to be joined and clamp into position. Make sure that all the glue that has been squeezed out of the joint is wiped away with a damp cloth. Check that the joint is square before allowing the glue to set.

5 Cut out the remaining wood in the hole with a mortise chisel and trim off the flat sides with a bevel-edge chisel, making sure that the ends and sides are exactly vertical and parallel.

7 Fit the joint together dry (without glue) and make any adjustments with a broad-bladed bevel-edge chisel until the joint is accurate.

HAUNCHED MORTISE AND TENON

This joint is most appropriately used at the top corner of a table or stool or similar construction. The purpose of the haunch is to provide contact in the mortise for the entire length of the tenon, thus adding strength to the joint.

What you will need – tools

- Bench with bench vice
- Try square
- Carpenter's pencil
- Tenon saw (back saw)
- Bevel-edge (paring) chisels
- Carpenter's wooden mallet
- Electric drill and drill bits
- G-clamps (C-clamps)
- Mortise gauge
- Firmer (framing) chisel or mortise chisel
- White wood glue
- Damp cloth

2 Set the two pins of the mortise gauge at exactly one-third and two-thirds of the width of the wood and, working from the face side on both pieces, mark the lines for the mortise hole and tenon cut. Draw in these lines with a pencil point to make the guides more visible.

3 Fix the wood in the bench vice (or clamp it to the work surface) and drill out the bulk of the mortise hole, using a drill bit about a millimetre (¹⁄₃₂ in) narrower than the completed hole should be. If you are using a hand-held electric drill, make sure that the drill is vertical to the wood.

4 Chop out the remaining wood with a firmer or mortise chisel, and trim the flat sides of the hole with a bevel-edge chisel. Also cut the slot for the haunch, making sure that the ends and sides are exactly vertical and parallel.

5 For the tenon section, use a tenon saw to cut down the wood on the scrap side of the tenon lines so that you have a completed tenon similar to the one in the photograph above. The haunch should be about 20% of the width of the tenon.

1 Establish exactly where the joint is to be made, and use the try square to draw square lines right around the wood.

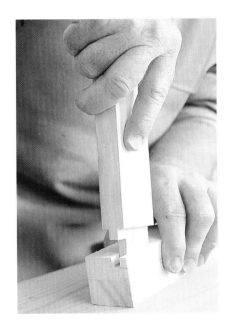

6 Fit the joint together dry (without glue) and make any adjustments with a firmer chisel so that the joint fits together without any gaps. When the joint is complete, apply glue to all the surfaces to be joined and clamp into position with G-clamps. Make sure that all the excess glue squeezed out of the joint is wiped away with a damp cloth. Check that the joint is square before leaving the glue to set.

BRIDLE JOINT

This joint can be used for the corners of frames as it is strong and very neat.

What you will need – tools

- Bench with bench vice
- Carpenter's pencil
- Try square
- Mortise gauge
- Tenon saw (back saw)
- G-clamps (C-clamps)
- Coping saw
- Broad and narrow firmer (framing) chisels
- White wood glue
- Damp cloth

1 Establish where the joint is to be constructed, and mark square lines right around both pieces of wood.

2 Set the mortise gauge to exactly one-third and two-thirds the thickness of the wood.

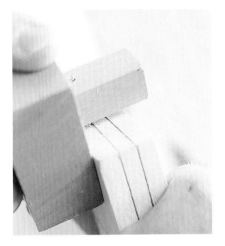

3 Working from the face side on each piece, use the mortise gauge to mark lines on the two edges and end of the wood.

4 'Hatch' in lines on the scrap areas to ensure that you do not make mistakes when you cut these out.

5 Secure one piece of wood in the bench vice and, using a tenon saw, cut out the tenon section of the joint.

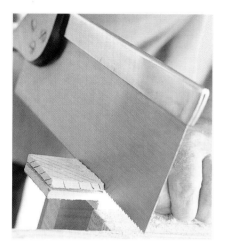

6 When these vertical lines have been cut, remove this piece from the bench vice, clamp it firmly to the bench surface and cut away the scrap on each side to establish the tenon.

7 Fix the other piece in the bench vice and, using a tenon saw, cut the vertical lines to establish the centre slot.

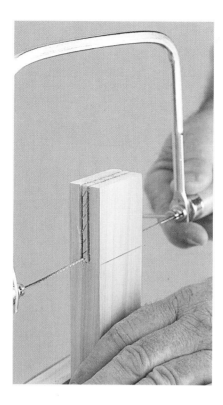

8 Use a coping saw to cut away the scrap in the centre slot.

9 Fix this same piece vertically in the bench vice, and clean up the slot with a broad firmer chisel on the flat side and a narrow chisel on the bottom of the slot until the slot is square and true.

10 Fit the joint dry (without glue) and make any necessary adjustments with a firmer chisel.

11 When complete, paint all contacting surfaces with glue, assemble the joint and clamp up using a G-clamp (don't forget the protective blocks and greaseproof paper). Before leaving the glue to set, use the try square to check that the joint is exactly square.

DOWEL JOINT

An alternative to the mortise and tenon joint is the dowel joint. It is quicker to make than a mortise and tenon, but it is not as strong. This joint can be used with projects where there will not be a great deal of pressure on the joint, for example a small coffee table.

1a Set the marking gauge to mark the position of the dowels on both pieces of wood. Remember to measure from the face side.

2 Use a nail punch to make an indentation where the dowel holes are to be drilled – this will aid accurate drilling.

1b It's also advisable to stagger the dowels (do not set them one above the other), as this will prevent the wood splitting along the grain when drilling or inserting the dowels.

3 Use a brad-point twist bit with the same diameter as the dowel rods. The drilled holes should never be wider than half the width of the wood, should be the same on each piece and, for thicker wood, such as table legs, should be about 20 mm (¾ in) deep. When drilling, make sure that the drill is held at a 90° angle to the wood.

4 Cut the required number of dowels 2 mm (⅟₁₆ in) shorter than the combined depth of the holes (if each hole is 20 mm/ ¾ in deep, each piece of dowel should be about 38 mm/1½ in long). Slightly taper both ends of each dowel using a rasp.

5a Tap the dowels dry (without glue) into one side and put the joint together dry to check that it fits well.

5b When you are satisfied that the joint is neat and accurate, apply glue onto one half of each dowel and put it into its required position. Paint wood glue onto all the surfaces that are going to be joined and clamp up the joint with a sash cramp. Excess glue should be wiped away with a damp cloth. Leave the joint to set for 24 hours.

HALVING (LAP) JOINT

This joint is made by removing half the width in the central section of one piece of wood and half the width of the top section of another piece of wood. These sections are joined together, maintaining the original thickness of a single piece of wood.

A halving joint is not very strong and should only be used for simple joints, such as those in a frame.

What you will need – tools

- Bench with bench vice
- Carpenter's pencil
- Try square
- Steel rule or retractable steel tape measure
- Tenon saw (back saw)
- G-clamps (C-clamps)
- Bevel-edge (paring) chisel
- White wood glue
- Damp cloth

1a Lay the two pieces together (one on top of the other in a T-shape) in the same position they will be when the joint is complete.

1b Make a pencil mark on either side of each section where they are in contact with each other.

2 Using the try square, draw pencil lines all the way around the sides and edges of both pieces.

3 Measure the thickness of each piece of wood (they should be the same), divide this exactly by two and set the marking gauge at this measurement.

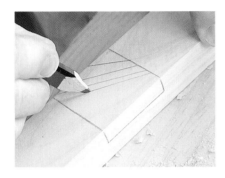

4 Working from the face side on one piece, mark the lines to indicate where you need to cut away the scrap and pencil in the indentations to make it more visible.

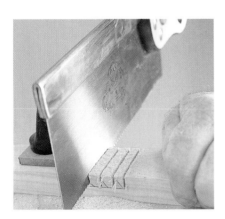

5 Secure the lower section of the cross piece to the work surface with G-clamps and, using a tenon saw, cut several vertical lines into the scrap wood down to the gauge line (half the depth of the wood).

6 Using a bevel-edge chisel, and working from both edges towards the middle, remove the scrap wood.

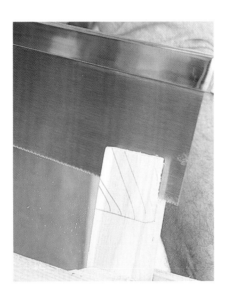

7 Fix the other piece vertically in the bench vice and, again using a tenon saw, cut down the length of the wood to the marked line.

8 Secure this same piece to the work surface in a horizontal position, and cut away the remainder of the scrap to create a completed tenon section.

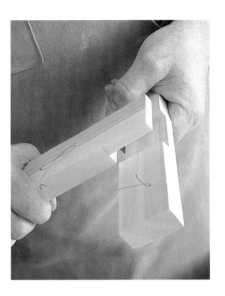

9 Check that the two pieces fit snugly together, and carefully make any adjustments with a bevel-edge chisel. When you are satisfied that the joint is as near perfect as possible, make the joint permanent using white wood glue. The finished joint should fit as accurately as the one in the photograph below.

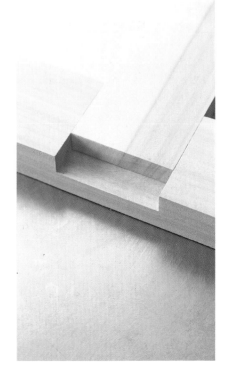

CORNER DOWEL JOINT

This joint is quicker and easier to make than a mortise and tenon joint, but it is not nearly as strong.

1 Secure the two sections in the bench vice in the same position as they will be when the joint is complete, and draw in marking lines where the sections come into contact with each other.

2 Mark the dowel positions on both pieces of wood. Select a drill bit that is the same diameter as the dowel you wish to use, and drill two 20 mm (¾ in) deep holes in the edge of one piece of wood.

3 Secure the other piece of wood in the bench vice and drill two identical holes into the end of this piece.

4 Cut the required number of dowels 2 mm (¹⁄₁₆ in) shorter than the combined depth of the holes (if each hole is 20 mm/¾ in deep, each piece of dowel should be about 38 mm/1½ in long). Slightly taper both ends of each dowel using a rasp.

5 Brush white wood glue onto one of the ends of each dowel and tap them into place with a mallet in one of the pieces of wood.

6 First making sure that there is no surplus glue on the surface, tap the joint together dry (without glue) as a trial fitting.

7 If the joint fits properly, take it apart again and brush glue onto all the surfaces that will meet. Rejoin the sections and clamp them with a sash cramp. Wipe away all surplus glue. The application of a clamp can pull a joint out of shape, so check all angles with a try square and make any necessary adjustments before leaving the glue to set.

DOVETAIL HALVING (SINGLE LAPPING DOVETAIL)

This joint is far stronger than a regular halving joint, as the wedge-shaped dovetail prevents the joint from pulling apart.

1 Mark a square line on all four sides of the end of one of the pieces to indicate the length of the dovetail.

2 Divide the thickness of one of the two pieces of wood exactly by two (they should be the same), and set a marking gauge at this thickness. (The line across the width should be the same as the width of the second piece.)

3 Using an adjustable bevel set to 30°, mark out the dovetail on both sides of this same piece.

4 Working from the face side, mark hatch lines to indicate where you need to cut away the scrap.

5 Securely fix the dovetail piece in the bench vice and cut down the scrap side with the tenon or dovetail saw.

6 Turn the piece of wood around and, using a tenon saw, cut away the scrap wood to leave a completed dovetail.

7 Lay the completed dovetail section on top of the other piece in the same position as the joint will be when it is complete. Mark out the dovetail with a sharp pencil where the two surfaces come into contact with each other.

8 Draw the vertical lines down the edges of the second piece with a try square.

10 Using a tenon saw, cut several vertical lines into the scrap wood down to the gauge line (half the depth of the wood).

11 Working from both edges towards the middle, use a bevel-edge chisel to remove the scrap wood.

12 Check that the two pieces fit snugly together, and make any necessary adjustments with a bevel-edge chisel. When you are satisfied that the joint is as near perfect as possible, apply glue to the surfaces to be joined and clamp the joint in position.

9 Mark the halfway line with the already set marking gauge (remember to start marking from the face side).

Joints for box construction

DOWEL JOINT

The major disadvantage of the dowel joint is that it has limited use because, structurally, it is not very strong and its strength is dependent upon all the surfaces being flat and square.

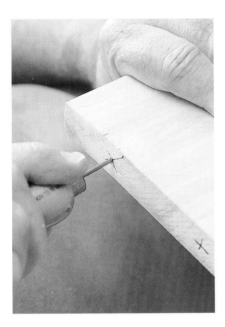

1 Mark out one piece of board showing the correct position of the completed joint. Mark the positions of the dowels – they should be about 20 mm (¾ in) in from each end and then about 100 mm (4 in) apart. A pencilled cross is adequate, but making an indentation at the centre point with a bradawl will give the drill bit a better starting point and will prevent the bit from slipping off the mark.

2 Clamp the two pieces to your work surface (with the flat sides together) and mark the dowel points on the other section of board so that the drilled holes will be in exactly the same position on each piece.

3 Using a drill bit the same thickness as the dowel and fitted with a depth stop, drill a hole into the end piece at every marked point. Make sure that the holes are in the centre of the width of the board and are 20 mm (¾ in) deep.

4 Using the same drill bit, set the depth stop to no more than three-quarters the thickness of the second board and drill the holes in this piece at the marked points.

5 Cut the required number of dowels to 2 mm (¹⁄₁₆ in) shorter than the combined depth of the holes, and dry-tap them into place to test the accuracy of the joint.

6 When you are satisfied that the joint is as near perfect as possible, make it permanent by applying glue on the dowels and on every surface that will be joined, and clamp up with a sash cramp.

STOPPED HOUSING (STOPPED DADO)

A stopped housing joint is strong and stable and is usually used to secure shelves into cabinets or bookcases (see also project three: room divider on pages 127–130).

(see also project three: room divider on pages 127–130).

What you will need – tools

- Bench with bench vice
- Carpenter's pencil
- Try square
- Marking gauge
- Tenon saw (back saw)
- Router
- Bevel-edge (paring) chisel
- Carpenter's wooden mallet
- G-clamps (C-clamps)
- Protective goggles
- White wood glue
- Damp cloth

1 Mark out the boards showing the intended position of the completed joint, and make sure that the lines are square across the board.

2 Using a marking gauge set to 30 mm (1¼ in) (or whatever your choice is, depending on the width of the boards), measure from the edge mark to determine where the stop will be on both boards.

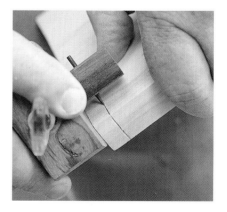

3 Decide on the depth of the housing (it should never be more than half the thickness of the receiving board) and, using a marking gauge set to this depth, mark the housing depth on the end of the board.

4 Cut away the scrap in the end piece with a tenon saw to form the stop.

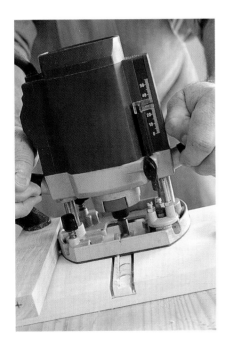

5 Using a router set to the required depth, rout out the bulk of the housing. To keep a straight line, this is best accomplished using a wooden strip clamped to the board as a guide.

6 Use a bevel-edge chisel to chop out the square end of the stop.

7 Test-fit the joint together dry and make any necessary adjustments. When the joint is accurate, apply glue to all surfaces that will be in contact with one another, and clamp up.

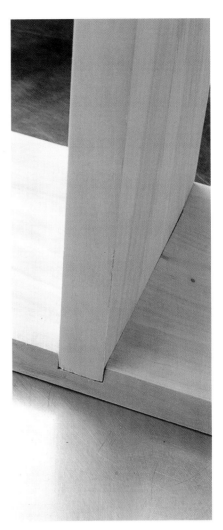

THROUGH DOVETAILS

This joint is used to secure the edges of box-type constructions, particularly drawers. It should not, however, be used on the front of drawers, as the end grain of the dovetails will show through.

1 Assuming that the boards to be joined are the same thickness, use a marking gauge set to the thickness of one board to mark around the ends of both boards as shown.

2 Calculate the size of the dovetails (this will depend on the width of the boards) and, using an adjustable bevel set at 30°, pencil in the dovetails on one side of the end of one board.

3 Secure this piece vertically in the bench vice and use the try square to draw the tail lines across the thickness of the board.

4 Again using the adjustable bevel, draw in the dovetails on the other side of the board, following the square lines from step 3 above.

5 Holding this piece firmly in the bench vice, cut out the vertical lines of the tails with a dovetail saw and then use the coping saw to cut the horizontal lines. It's always a good idea to 'hatch' in the scrap pieces as this prevents cutting out the wrong section, which, surprisingly enough, is quite easy to do!

6 Fix the other piece in the bench vice and draw along the tails to give the position of the pins.

7 Cut out the pins in the same way as the tails were cut in step 5.

8 Test-fit the joint together dry and make any necessary adjustments. When you are satisfied that the joint is accurate, apply white wood glue to all touching surfaces and clamp up. Check that the joint is square before leaving the glue to set for 24 hours.

Joints for long boards

TONGUE-AND-GROOVE

This is a very strong and effective way of joining boards together, the only real drawback being that the joint is visible on the ends of the boards.

4 Use a spindle cutter, table saw or radial arm saw to cut away the two sides of the other board to form the tongue of the joint.

1 Set the pins of the mortise gauge at exactly one-third and two-thirds the thickness of one of the boards.

2 Mark in the lines from the face side of both boards.

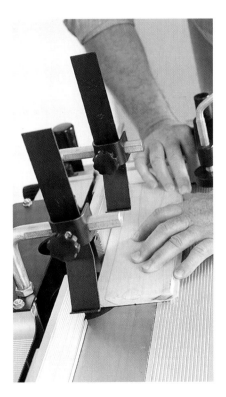

3 Use a spindle cutter, table saw or radial arm saw with a cutting guide and cut out a groove that is 10 mm (⅜ in) deep on one board.

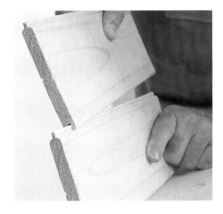

5 Test-fit the joint dry (without glue) and make any necessary adjustments. When the joint is complete, apply glue to every surface that will meet, and clamp up.

DOWEL JOINT

This is a very quick and straightforward method of joining long boards, but it is not as strong as a tongue-and-groove or biscuit joint.

What you will need – tools

- Bench with bench vice
- Carpenter's pencil
- Try square
- Marking gauge
- Bradawl
- Electric drill and drill bits
- Tenon saw (back saw)
- Rasp.
- White wood glue
- Sash cramp (bar clamp)
- Damp cloth

1 Hold the two boards together in a bench vice so that the edges to be joined are next to each other.

2 Mark the position of the dowels (about 10 mm/⅜ in in from each end and about 100 mm/4 in apart) and use a try square to mark these lines across the thickness of both boards.

3 Remove the boards from the bench vice and, using a marking gauge, mark a line down the middle of the thickness of the boards so that the dowel holes will be exactly in the centre. Make an indentation at the centre point of each spot with a bradawl to establish a good starting point for the drill bit.

4 Using a drill bit the same thickness as the dowels and fitted with a depth stop, drill holes 20 mm (¾ in) deep at every marked point.

5 Cut the required number of dowels 2 mm (¹⁄₁₆ in) shorter than the combined depth of the opposing holes, in this case 38 mm (1½ in) long, and taper the ends with a rasp.

6 Assemble the joint dry to ensure a good fit, and make any necessary adjustments. When complete, make the joint permanent by applying white wood glue to every touching surface and clamp up.

BISCUIT JOINT

This is probably the most popular joint used today for joining long boards. A biscuit jointer can be very expensive, but a spindle cutter or even a hand-held router can be used to cut the grooves. The strength of this joint is provided by the biscuit, which absorbs the glue and expands slightly into the joint, making a very tight and strong fit.

1 Hold the two boards together in a bench vice so that the edges to be joined are next to each other.

2 Mark the position of the centre of the biscuits, about 70 mm (2¾ in) in from each end and about 300–400 mm (12–16 in) apart (this will depend on the length of the boards). Use a square to mark these lines across the thickness of both boards.

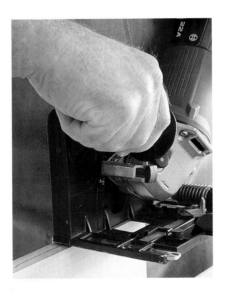

3 Use the biscuit jointer (set to 2 mm (¹⁄₁₆ in) deeper than half the width of the biscuit) to cut a slot exactly in the centre of the width of the boards at each of these points, to accommodate the full length of the biscuits. To save time, although it weakens the joint slightly, a long groove can be cut in each board, but don't continue the grooves right through the ends of the boards. This is the only real solution if you don't have access to a biscuit jointer.

4 Tap dry biscuits into the slots, and tap the joint together to ensure that it fits well. When you are satisfied that the joint is as near perfect as possible, apply glue to the biscuits and all touching surfaces, and clamp up with a sash cramp.

Woodturning

Is the woodworker an artist or an artisan? When it comes to woodturning the argument usually falls to the arts side, as nothing quite compares with setting a piece of prepared wood on your lathe and then watching as it changes in shape and size under the careful movement of your own hand. Woodturning enables you to create something beautiful and personal, and you are limited only by the extent of your imagination.

LATHES

An early lathe

The full history of woodturning is lost in the mists of time, but there are drawings on record of craftsmen working primitive pole lathes, which consisted of the piece of wood to be turned secured between two centre points. A leather thong was bound around the end of the wood and then secured between a green sapling still planted in the ground and a treadle under the bench. The power for this lathe was supplied by the craftsman's foot and the springy sapling.

Fortunately we've come a long way since then, but, strange as it may seem, there has recently been a resurgence of interest in ancient tools and methods, and woodworkers are going out to find saplings to bend and use in pole lathes, emulating those used 300 years ago, just for the fun of it!

Electric drill attachment

One of the least expensive methods of beginning a career in turning is by buying a lathe attachment for an electric drill, where the drill provides the power source. Although relatively inexpensive, the disadvantage is that, unless you have a variable-speed drill, you are strictly limited with regard to turning speed. Another disadvantage is that poor-quality electric drills tend to wobble, which can lead to unsatisfactory results.

Home craftsmen's lathes

There are a variety of lathes available that fall into this category. Some of these lathes are mass-produced in Eastern countries, are relatively

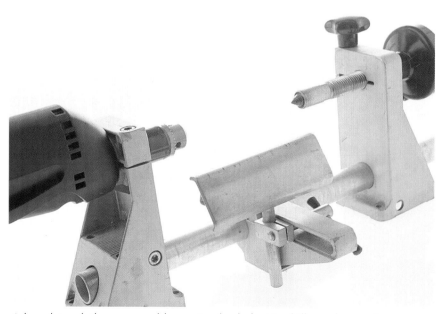

A bench-top lathe powered by a standard electric drill can be used to create small turned items, such as table lamps or small bowls.

inexpensive and are usually a perfectly adequate tool with which to get started.

There are other lathes in this category manufactured by well-known European and American companies, which are of a higher quality, both in materials and engineering, and are therefore more expensive. If you are interested in honing your skills as a woodturner, this type of lathe would be the one to aim for.

The models available include those that can be clamped or screwed to the bench, or others that are freestanding – your choice will be governed by availability of workshop space as well as finances.

Lathe parts
There are basically only five major parts to a lathe:

1. Stand – should be sturdy and well constructed.

2. Motor (headstock) – attached to a gearing mechanism with rubber belts.

3. Driving centre – attached to the motor with belts.

4. Back centre (tailstock centre) – the passive end on which the wood turns.

5. Tool rest – can be adjusted in height and distance from the spinning wood.

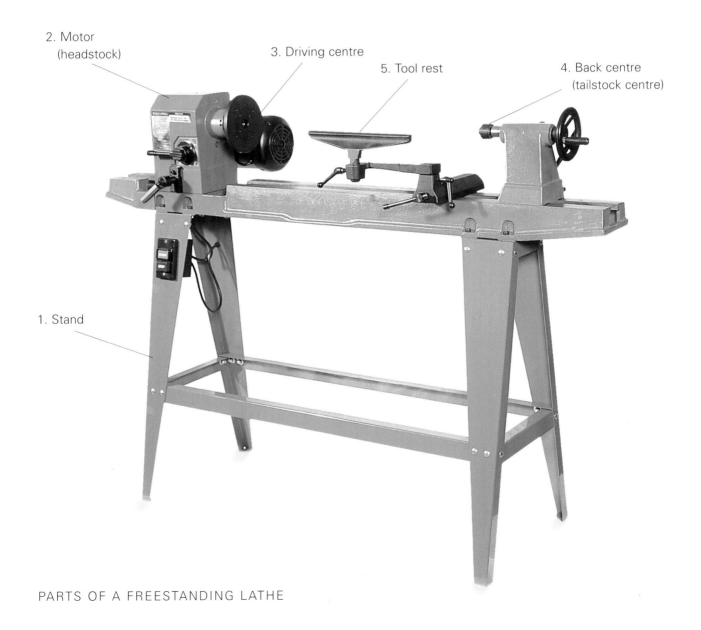

2. Motor (headstock)

3. Driving centre

5. Tool rest

4. Back centre (tailstock centre)

1. Stand

PARTS OF A FREESTANDING LATHE

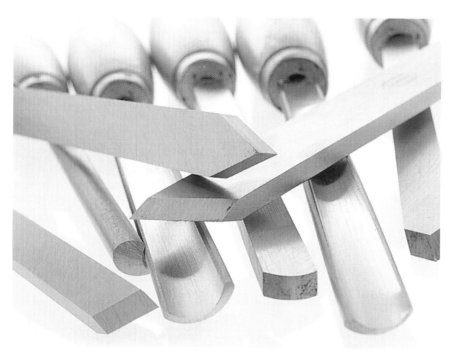

Lathe chisels (turning tools)

There are two types of chisel for use on the lathe. One is called a scraper chisel, which describes its action, and the other is the cutting chisel.

An adequate set of lathe chisels will comprise six or eight chisels with blades of various shapes and sizes. The handles of lathe chisels are longer and more shapely than ordinary woodworking chisels. These handles allow the craftsman a firm grip and good control of the tool while shaping the wood, which is turning on the lathe. The other major difference is in the shapes of the cutting edges, as can be seen in the photograph.

For the general woodworker, a set of about six or eight lathe chisels should be sufficient to create the variety of shapes used in woodturning.

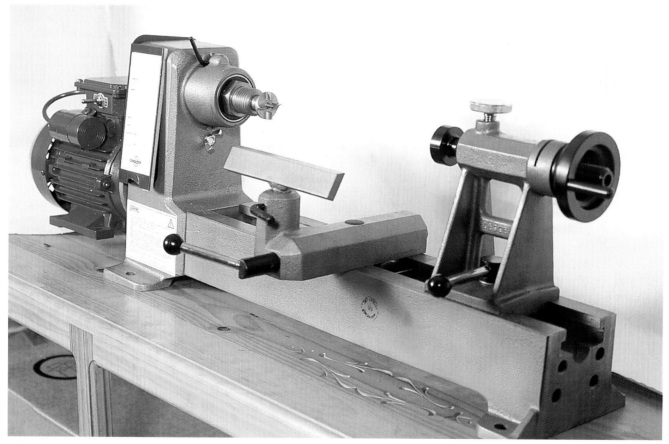

Choose a lathe that is suited to your purposes and available workshop space. The portable bench-top model pictured here should be adequate for most turning projects, and can be packed away when not in use.

Never use lathe chisels as ordinary chisels – they are specialized tools, and one little tap with a mallet will probably shatter the handle (as I found out as a youngster, resulting in a destroyed lathe chisel and a wallop from my dad!).

Much of the work done on a lathe will be with spindles, that is to say, shaping a piece of wood that is centred between two points, for example table legs or lamp stands.

A face plate can be attached to the lathe drive shaft for turning bowls.

Sometimes, such as when turning bowls, the back centre cannot be used as it would prevent access to the inside surface. In this instance, the wood to be turned is screwed firmly onto a face plate, which in turn is screwed onto the drive shaft of the lathe. The now redundant back centre assembly should be removed to facilitate movement at the face of the bowl.

MEASURING TOOLS FOR LATHE WORK

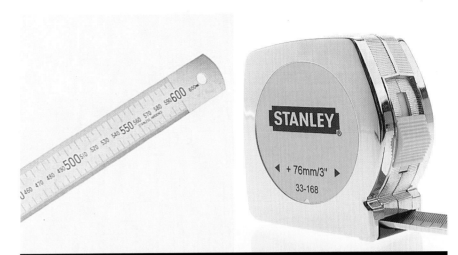

Steel rule   **Retractable steel tape measure**

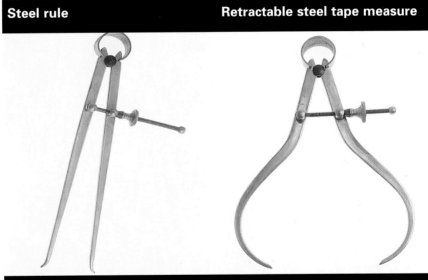

Internal calliper   **External calliper**

Measuring tools

Apart from a steel rule or retractable steel tape measure, you will need three other basic measuring tools: internal callipers, external callipers and dividers. These are about the only tools with which you can make accurate measurements on lathe work, and they are used to check the diameters of the convex and concave curves created on the lathe.

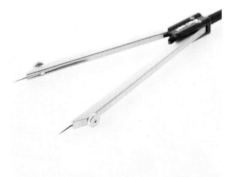

Dividers

Before you attempt a 'proper' turning project, it is a good idea to try some experimental work. Here's a start:

1 Choose a piece of wood about 300 mm (12 in) long and fix it vertically in the bench vice. Draw in diagonal lines at one end to establish the exact centre. Place a nail punch on this centre point and give it a light tap with a hammer so that it is firmly established. Repeat this at the other end.

2 Before taking the wood out of the vice, measure 10 mm (⅜ in) from each corner on each side. Make a clear pencil mark and draw these lines across the corners and down the entire length of the piece of wood. This area needs to be planed away, so that when you turn the wood on the lathe there will be no sharp corners to jam on the chisel or fly off in large chunks.

3 Centre the wood on the lathe. The method of setting will vary from lathe to lathe, but ensure that the wood is firmly established on the driving centre and that the back centre is secure. Set the speed of the lathe according to the manufacturer's instructions, but generally it should be about 1 500 rpm for uneven wood and about 2 000 rpm for finishing off.

4 Check that all locking nuts are tight, and put on your protective goggles.

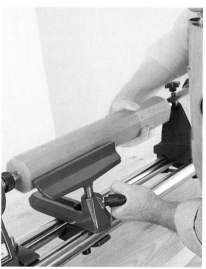

5 Set the tool rest as close as possible to the wood and about 5 mm (³⁄₁₆ in) below the centre. Before switching on the lathe, turn the wood by hand to ensure that it turns freely without touching the tool rest.

6 Stand to the side of the lathe and switch it on. If the wood turns easily without wobbling, touching the tool rest, or flying off (which is why you stand to the side of the lathe!), you are ready to begin.

10 Take the chisel away and switch off the lathe. When it has completely stopped, examine the effect of your efforts.

11a Following steps 7 to 10 above, try to turn a perfect cylinder on the wood; that is, completely round, and with parallel sides over its entire length.

7 Take a round nose chisel or shallow gouge and, holding the handle at the end in your writing hand and the blade shaft firmly in the other hand with an overhand grip (about 50 mm (2 in) from the cutting edge), offer the chisel, horizontal to the ground, very carefully to the wood. The chisel should rest as flat as possible on the tool rest.

8 Don't put too much pressure on the chisel as this could stop the lathe, jam the wood or, in the most serious case, cause the wood to split and fly off the lathe. Use the chisels gently until you get the feel of how they will perform. Continue your cut along the length of the wood, or as far as the tool rest will allow you to.

9 Watch with delight as the first layers begin to peel away. Don't worry about a little vibration at this stage, as the wood will be unevenly balanced as it spins. Only when a cylinder has been formed and there are no unbalanced areas left will it turn smoothly.

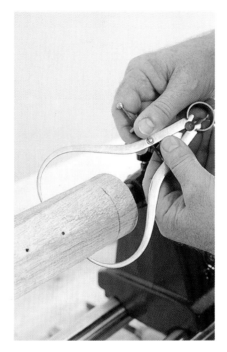

11b At each stop, use the callipers to check the uniformity of the diameter. To achieve an accurate cylinder you will have to stop and start the lathe a number of times to examine your progress.

12 When you have achieved the perfect cylinder, start at the end nearest the motor and experiment with a concave curve. Also experiment with differently shaped chisels, stopping frequently to examine your progress.

13 When you've finished all that you want to try with the chisels, use various sandpapers to get the feel of finishing off a job. But be careful – remove the tool rest when using sandpaper to prevent your hand from accidentally getting drawn into it. Abrasive papers can also get very hot if they are held too hard against the wood. Hold them lightly and move up and down along the entire length – this will prevent scratches being indented into the wood.

chapter four

finishes and finishing

For a project to look really good when it has been completed depends on the way that it has been finished. As woodwork has developed, both professionally and as a hobby, so the technical quality of wood finishes has increased along with it.

Most of the finishes described in this chapter are practical and so widely used today, but a few belong largely to the realm of the specialist and are not used too often by the hobbyist. That is not to say that the finish they produce is not good when applied properly, but just that over the past few decades, and even centuries, advances in chemistry have provided some excellent finishes that make their predecessors look a little outdated. Trying the older methods on one or two projects, however, will give enormous pleasure when the results are better than you expected.

Preparing the surface

The way in which the wood's surface is prepared prior to the application of the chosen finish is vital, as a clean and smooth surface is the most important basis for a good-quality and durable finish.

It's worth remembering that anything that remains on the surface of the wood will prevent the finish from penetrating the surface and will result in unsightly patches on the finished product. Examples of what can be left on the surface include the residue of wood glue squeezed out of joints, or traces of paint, varnish, oil, wax and other finishes left behind when restoring a piece of furniture.

The problem of excess water-based white wood glue can easily be solved by ensuring that when joints are put together, any excess glue squeezed out of the joint is wiped away thoroughly before the glue sets. Waterproof glues can be very difficult to clean away without leaving any effects – rather apply slightly less glue so that little or no residue is squeezed out when the joint is clamped.

Another point to take note of is that most of the preparation work on new surfaces should be accomplished prior to the joints being glued together. The reason for this is that some of the angles created by completed joints make it very difficult to access that area with sandpaper.

Some details regarding the types of sandpaper available are to be found in the chapter on tools (see pages 51–52), but it's probably worth repeating here that, for the purposes of the general woodworker and hobbyist, only three or four grades of sandpaper are really necessary: a coarse paper of about 80 grit, a medium paper of about 100 grit and then a very fine paper of about 400 grit – or even down to 1 200 grit for a glass-like finish.

Most of the hard work will have been done when you have completed the preparation and are ready to move on to the final finishing, but there are still a few things that need to be taken into account.

Inspecting the surface

Hold the wood in such a way so that you can see along the entire length and width of the surface, and so that as much light as possible reflects off the wood. By doing this you should be able to detect any undulations in the surface, such as ledges left by plane blades. You can also run your fingers and the palm of your hand across the surface to detect any unevenness.

Catching the light at just the right angle will show up any problems or imperfections on the surface.

When any undulations are discovered, corrective action should be taken by hand, or by the gentle use of a belt sander or orbital sander (using a medium paper), until you are satisfied that the surface is as you want it. Careful inspection with the hand and eye may also reveal other unwanted blemishes, such as holes around a knot in the timber, small cracks or splits in the surface, and joints which, in spite of your best endeavours, have not pulled together completely, leaving small gaps. All these problems can

Gaps, holes or cracks in the surface should be filled with matching wood filler. Once dry, the filler should be sanded flush with the surface.

be rectified by carefully filling the offending holes with wood filler. The wood filler should be applied with a putty knife or similar instrument and packed in tightly until it is slightly proud of the surface, and should then be left to dry for 24 hours. When completely dry, the wood filler should be sanded until it is flush with the surrounding wood.

When satisfied with all the surfaces of the project, the final preparation can be completed by resanding every surface with a very fine sandpaper. Always sand with the grain of the timber and never across it, as this could leave scratches that may be difficult to remove. Sharp edges and corners can also be gently rounded by using fine sandpaper.

When you have completed the final sanding, inspect the entire project again, both visually and by touch. Only when the surfaces are absolutely smooth and clean will you be ready to apply the chosen surface finish.

Proficient woodworkers should have brushes of several different widths at their disposal. The quality of the brushes is of paramount importance – the use of cheap brushes results in poor finishes.

Inaccuracies are almost inevitable for most woodworkers. The application of an appropriate wood filler can be an effective solution.

Brushes

Many finishing materials are best applied with a brush, and the quality and care of the brush is very important to ensure a good finish.

When buying paintbrushes from a hardware store, there will usually be a selection of two or three qualities from which to choose. Check the quality and firmness of the bristles in the sleeve and the firmness with which the bristles and their sleeve are attached to the handle.

Poor quality brushes usually have coarse bristles and have an uneven shape and tip – this will leave brush marks on the surface instead of a smooth finish. If the sleeve is not firmly attached to the handle, this could fall off in the middle of an application of varnish or paint, which does nothing for your stress levels, let alone the finish! Also, when using one of these cheaper brushes the bristles tend to fall out and lodge themselves in the middle of the surface you're trying to perfect, causing even more frustration. Inevitably, this usually happens on the last finishing touch of the brush stroke!

A good quality brush will give a smooth finish because the bristles are fine and tapered, and the head is unlikely to detach itself from the handle because of the quality of the materials. If properly cared for, the brush will last a great deal longer than its less expensive counterpart. In fact, an expensive brush will probably be more economical than a cheap one, as the finishes and longevity will be well worth the extra cost. Inbetween applying coats, the brush should be placed in a container of turpentine (mineral spirits), thinners or water (depending on the base of the finish with which you're working). The solution should be deep enough to completely cover the bristles. When the brush is needed again, the excess liquid can be shaken out and the brush dried on a soft, clean cloth. (It's helpful to have a supply of containers in which to clean and store brushes. Cutting off the lower half of plastic softdrink bottles provides excellent holders for this purpose at no cost.)

When you have finished using the brush, the bristles should be thoroughly washed in the appropriate cleaning material: water for water-based paints, turpentine (mineral spirits) for oil-based paints and varnishes, or thinners for spirit-based materials. Wash each brush at least twice and then wash it again in very hot water mixed with a liberal helping of dishwashing liquid. When you're sure that there are no traces of the original material on the brush, rinse it with clean, cold water, shake off the excess and hang it up to dry.

Pad applicators
In the application of most finishes, pads are a suitable alternative to brushes. Pads can be purchased ready-made, but the best pads are home-made from a soft, lint-free cloth, folded several times until a thick, flat surface is created. Another alternative is to use an old pair of pantihose with a wad of cotton wool inside.

The major benefits of pads over brushes is that they cost far less, they can be disposed of after use and they do not leave brush marks, although it does take a little practice to use a pad successfully. Inbetween applications, while waiting for the surface to dry, the pad can be securely wrapped in a plastic bag from which as much air as possible has been squeezed out. This will prevent the pad drying out and will enable you to use it again even after a few hours.

One of the disadvantages of using a home-made pad applicator is that unless you wear some protective covering on your hands, such as disposable rubber gloves, it can be a very messy business

How to prevent a brush from drying out

Pad applicators

A pad applicator in use

in terms of the residue left on your hands. Not only is this residue inconvenient and difficult to remove, but it can actually damage the skin. Rubber gloves can be quite expensive, but placing a plastic bag over your hand is just as effective and far less costly.

FINISHES

Guidelines to follow when

applying finishes:

- Almost every form of furniture finish or paint gives off fumes, some of which may be dangerous if inhaled in large doses, and others which are simply unpleasant. Ensure that your working area is well ventilated before starting the finishing process.

- As well as being sufficiently ventilated, your working area should be free of airborne dust and sheltered from the wind or draughts. Particles in the air, either remaining from the sanding process or being blown into the working area, can adhere to and blemish your otherwise beautiful surface.

- Although many finishes claim to be quick-drying, allow at least 24 hours drying time before sanding the surface in preparation for the application of the next coat.

Surface sealers

The surface of most woods is porous and will therefore absorb whatever liquid is applied to it. This characteristic can make finishing quite difficult as a number of coats may need to be applied before the finish begins to take any visible effect. For this reason, a sealer is often used in order to seal these pores and present a non-porous surface for the chosen finish.

In days gone by, sealer was made from finely ground plaster of Paris mixed with water, which was then rubbed into the surface. Today's wood sealers are more technologically advanced and can be bought in liquid form from your local hardware store. These are simply brushed onto the porous surface, following the manufacturer's instructions, and when totally dry are given a light sanding before the chosen finish is applied.

Wood fillers

Sometimes the colour of a wood filler is not a good match with the colour of the wood which it needs to fill. When this occurs, it's worth spending a little time experimenting in order to achieve a satisfactory solution. This can be achieved by mixing different colours of filler (preferably from the same manufacturer) until you achieve the required shade. Filler often darkens slightly as it dries, so smear some of your mixture on a piece of scrap wood from your project to see if the colour is compatible.

Different colour wood fillers can be used directly from the container or mixed together to match the colour of the wood surface.

Wood stains

Polyurethane varnish

Dilute with turpentine

Applying the first coat of polyurethane

Wood stains

It often occurs that the colour of the wood you use for a project does not match the surrounding décor or have the desired look, and this is where wood stains come into their own. Most manufacturers offer a range of 10–15 different wood stain colours – if they are from the same manufacturer, you can usually mix them to achieve the exact colour you need. Before applying the stain to the project, however, test the colour on a piece of scrap left over from the project. Only when this is completely dry will you be able to determine whether you have a match.

Stains can be applied with a brush or pad, but the most important factor is to make sure that you achieve an even and smear-free finish. Try not to overlap the same area more than 30 seconds after the first layer has been applied – this effectively constitutes a second coat which will be darker than the surrounding area.

Although most wood stains are spirit-based and therefore dry quickly, it is advisable to wait 24 hours before applying a second coat (if necessary). This will ensure that the last coat is completely dry.

Unlike paints and varnishes, wood stain does not need to be sanded down inbetween applications.

Polyurethane varnish

This is probably the most popular of all finishes used commercially and by the hobbyist. Polyurethane is impervious to water and other ordinary household spillages, and can also tolerate a fair amount of heat, therefore providing good surface protection as well as an attractive appearance.

Polyurethane can be purchased in a variety of colours as well as clear or neutral (natural). Although the latter will darken the surface of most woods by a shade or two, it will still provide the most natural-looking finish. Most polyurethane varnishes are available in a matt or high-gloss finish, although the matt is never really dull, but is similar to an eggshell finish.

A further choice is between exterior or interior quality. The exterior quality is suitable for window frames, flashings and garden furniture, whereas the interior is perfectly adequate for furniture that is unlikely to be used outside the home.

Three coats of polyurethane are usually sufficient, but for heavy-duty surfaces such as tabletops, a fourth coat will provide extra protection as well as a better-looking finish.

How to apply a polyurethane finish

1 When you are satisfied with the preparation of the surface of the wood, pour a measured quantity of polyurethane into a clean, empty container. Dilute the polyurethane by 10% with turpentine (mineral spirits) and stir thoroughly.

It's worth noting here that there are two reasons for pouring the polyurethane into a separate container in order to thin it down. The first is

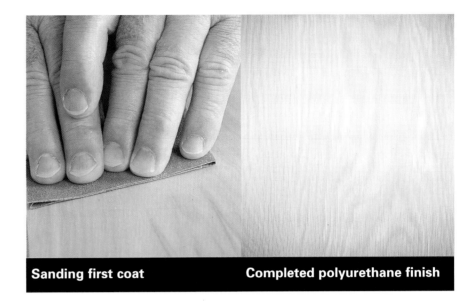

Sanding first coat   **Completed polyurethane finish**

quite obvious, because if 10% turpentine (mineral spirits) is poured into the original full container, it will overflow. The second reason is that the addition of turpentine (mineral spirits) will drastically reduce the shelf life of the diluted polyurethane and, unless used in the immediate future (certainly within 24 hours), you may find your expensive polyurethane becoming more like jelly than a furniture finish and therefore suitable only for the dustbin.

2 When the polyurethane is diluted, use a clean, soft paintbrush or pad applicator to apply the finish to the surface of the wood. Always brush with the grain and apply sparingly. If the application is to a vertical surface, using small amounts will make sure that the polyurethane does not drip or run. Before leaving the first coat to dry, ensure that no drips have accumulated on the underside of any of the surfaces due to gravitational pull. These drips should be

gently brushed into the surface (make sure that as much as possible of the polyurethane varnish has been squeezed out of the brush).

3 Although many of the polyurethane finishes are quick-drying, allow at least 24 hours drying time to ensure a solid finish.

4 The first coat of varnish will probably raise the surface of the grain of the wood as the varnish soaks into it, so don't be disappointed when the result is a rough surface and not a smooth one. When dry, use a very fine sandpaper to sand all surfaces – sand with the grain.

5 Inspect the entire surface, visually and by touch, to ensure that every part has been sanded smooth. When this has been done you will be ready to apply the next coat.

6 Repeat steps 2 to 5 until you achieve the require finish. Do not sand the final coat.

Wax

Waxing is probably the oldest form of wood sealing known to man, and has been used since it was discovered that rubbing beeswax into the surface of wood made it look better and gave it some protection against liquids. Several waxes are available on the market today, including beeswax, paraffin wax and carnauba, all sold mainly in solid form.

Wax is very easy to apply as all you need to do is use a pad or cloth to rub the solid wax onto the surface and then, with a firm circular movement, rub it thoroughly into the surface. This process is then repeated as many times as is necessary to get the finish you want. Waxing is very hard work indeed and you may end up with forearms like Popeye's, but the end result can be very, very beautiful.

Waxing, however, does have some disadvantages. It is not totally impervious to water, and liquid can penetrate the wax and discolour the wood underneath. Another disadvantage is that it needs to be renewed regularly, and although it may look beautiful, over the years the wax build-up can become so thick that it is easily scratched and disfigured. In fact, at this stage, even the mild warmth of a coffee mug or teacup can melt the wax and leave a permanent, unsightly stain.

To remove stains, the entire surface should be scraped down and the wax reapplied from scratch. Unfortunately, it is too late at this stage to use a polyurethane varnish instead,

Wax

Rubbing in a wax finish

Oils

Stroking in an oil finish

as the wax will have soaked so deeply into the surface that it will prevent the polyurethane from penetrating and drying.

Oils

Oils are not used very often in modern furniture finishing, mainly due to the several disadvantages of this method. For example, oil requires the application of many coats in order to achieve a good finish, it takes a long time to dry completely, and it can also

'weep'. Weeping occurs when the oil is either forced out of the wood by a natural process or remains on the surface without soaking in – this can lead to unsightly marks and possible damage to tablecloths or clothing. Perhaps the greatest disadvantage is that oils do not provide sufficient protection against water marks.

However, there are some advantages when it comes to using oil, as it is very easy to apply and, when applied

French polish and pad applicator

Sealing the surface with weak plaster of Paris mixture

Applying French polish evenly across the surface

today, as modern synthetic finishes are much easier to apply and are more durable. The skill of French polishing is practised mainly by professional antique restorers when a very old piece of furniture has become damaged or needs surface restoration.

Having said all this, French polishing is a skill that can be learned and enjoyed, and your experience as a woodworker is not complete until you've really had a go at this one. Do not despair, but persevere – although French polishing is a highly skilled technique, there's no reason why you can't achieve good results through knowledge and a little practice.

There are many different techniques and rules for applying French polish, but the liquid polish itself and the basic application technique are very simple indeed. The liquid is made up of a mixture of shellac (derived from the shell of the coca laca beetle) and methylated spirits (methyl alcohol), and while it is possible to buy shellac flakes from your local woodwork or hardware store, and to make it youself, it is much simpler to purchase the ready-made mixture.

Surface preparation is vitally important as far as French polishing is concerned. Sand the surface thoroughly, working through different grades of paper down to the finest possible silicone-based paper that you can obtain.

To seal the surface of the wood, mix some plaster of Paris with water (or use wood filler) and gently rub it into the

properly, it can provide a beautiful finish. In fact, the application is so simple that all you need to do is spread the oil on top of the surface and allow it to soak in until thoroughly dry. The surface residue is then wiped away with the same rag you used to apply the oil. Because oils are combustible, the cloth you use should be disposed of safely.

The most commonly used oil for furniture finishing is linseed oil, which can be purchased in liquid form.

French polish
Many woodworking hobbyists are frightened away from any attempt at French polishing due to the mystique which seems to surround this subject. Most woodworkers wouldn't attempt to achieve the almost perfect finish we see on a grand piano, for example, which looks as if somebody has embedded a sheet of glass into the surface of the wood.

French polishing was very popular during the Victorian era, but it is seldom used surface. Leave to dry then sand the surface again with the finest grit sandpaper available. Make sure that the surface is totally dust-free before attempting to apply the polish.

When applying French polish, ensure that your work area is warm, dry and totally dust-free. Ideally, this process should be carried out in a place different from your usual workshop where there is likely to be sawdust suspended in the atmosphere, which will inevitably end up on the beautiful surface. The liquid polish is applied to the wood surface with a pad, which in

French polishing is called a rubber. The rubber can be made from a soft, clean, lint-free cotton cloth, which is wrapped around some soft material wadding (an old woollen sock works well) to create a flat surface.

The application of the polish will be made easier by the addition of a few drops of linseed oil onto the surface of the rubber. Pour a little of the French polish onto the surface of the rubber and, using long strokes with the grain, apply it as evenly as possible to the surface. Try not to go over the same section again before it

has dried, as this will have an adverse effect on the finish.

Allow the polish to dry completely before applying the next coat and, after every two or three coats, rub down the surface with a very fine silicone paper. Make sure that all residual dust is removed from the surface with a clean duster before applying the next coat.

It may be necessary to apply eight or 10 coats before you begin to feel anywhere near satisfied with the finish, but don't despair – the end result is very satisfying, especially as you develop your own degree of expertise.

A lime-wash finish can be an interesting and contemporary alternative to conventional finishes such as paint or varnish.

Lime wash

'Lime wash' is actually a misnomer, as this finish does not contain lime and it is not washed on, but the technique is probably called this because the finished article has a similar appearance to a lime-washed wall.

This finishing method has become very popular in recent years, and you can often see furniture finished in a variety of colours. Many purists will frown upon any finish that disguises the natural beauty of wood, but if the lime wash is applied correctly it will highlight the grain and characteristics of the wood, unlike paint, which totally covers it.

The successful application of this finish is dependent on the wood surface being absolutely clean – lime wash will not take well to a surface that has been previously treated unless every trace of the last finish has been eradicated.

But first, a warning. Make sure that the area in which you apply this finish is very well ventilated, as inhalation of the paint and thinners fumes can be very unpleasant and hazardous to your health.

The base material commonly used is automotive paint, thinned right down with lacquer thinners. The mix can be anything from one measure of paint to ten measures of thinners, or up to 1:30, depending on the degree of translucency you wish to achieve. The strength of the mix will also depend on the colour used and the effect you want, and the only way to

Although not preferred by most woodworkers, paint can be a colourful and durable option for finishing wooden items.

achieve a satisfactory result is to experiment on pieces of scrap wood, applying the liquid by brush, rag, roller or even spray. It's a good idea to keep a record of your experiments, noting the colour, proportions of the mix, the wood it was used on and your impressions of the result. This will be a good reference for future use when you can avoid wasting time by mixing combinations that you may have tried before.

When you are satisfied with the colour and the effect on the scrap wood, the mixture can be applied to the piece of woodwork. Only one coat is required, as all the pores of the wood will be sealed by the automotive paint and nothing will be able to penetrate the surface after that. When thoroughly dry, the surface can be sealed with clear varnish or polyurethane.

Paint

In the writer's opinion, the application of paint to wood should be discouraged as this totally conceals the natural beauty of the timber, but occasionally a pleasant effect can be achieved by painting a particular area of a piece to contrast with the wood and complement the whole.

Before painting, the surface should be well prepared and free of any dust or oil.

Paint is usually applied with a brush, and an undercoat of matt (usually white) should be applied first.

When the undercoat is completely dry (leave it for at least 24 hours), sand the surface thoroughly with a fine paper, as the undercoat will raise the grain of the wood to a rough finish. Apply the top coats (usually two) and sand down the surface inbetween each coat.

chapter five

step-by-step projects

Now comes the opportunity to put theory, knowledge and learned skills to the test! By this stage of the book you should have a broader understanding of the raw material, have achieved an enhanced technical knowledge of the tools and techniques, and have had some practice working with wood.

All your acquired knowledge and skill can now be successfully applied to the projects described here. At first glance these may seem a little ambitious, but take heart – although impressive, they are certainly not beyond the scope of someone who can use what has been learned so far. Our goal is to take you beyond the 'run-of-the-mill' coffee table and help you create something really useful and challenging.

The dining table involves only three basic joints – the chair is reasonably straightforward and is designed to complement the table. The bedside cabinet looks really good and involves a simple drawer construction that can be applied to any other project requiring drawers. The room divider may seem large, but its simple construction enables you to create a piece of furniture which, being mobile, has many applications in the contemporary home or office. And the little tripod table will give you the chance to practise the skill of wood turning, as well as the opportunity to use a router, jigsaw and a simple home-made tool.

So, take up the challenge and enjoy creating something you previously may have considered beyond your ability – you can do it!

PROJECT ONE: TURNED TRIPOD TABLE

The centre post and legs of the photographed table are made from kiaat, but mahogany or any other attractive red or dark wood can be used. The top is made from oak.

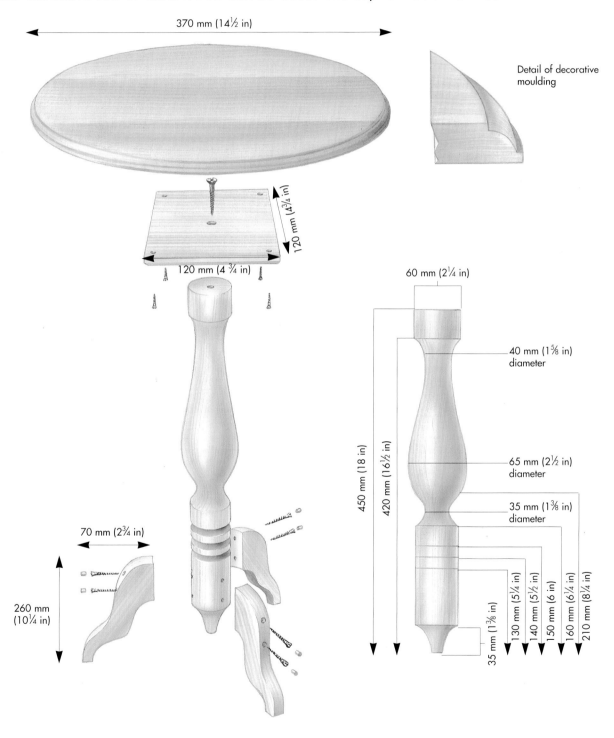

370 mm (14½ in)

Detail of decorative moulding

120 mm (4¾ in)

120 mm (4¾ in)

60 mm (2¼ in)

40 mm (1⅝ in) diameter

65 mm (2½ in) diameter

35 mm (1⅜ in) diameter

450 mm (18 in)

420 mm (16½ in)

70 mm (2¾ in)

260 mm (10¼ in)

35 mm (1⅜ in)

130 mm (5¼ in)

140 mm (5½ in)

150 mm (6 in)

160 mm (6¼ in)

210 mm (8¼ in)

- 1 piece of kiaat 70 x 70 x 500 mm (2¾ x 2¾ x 20 in) (for the centre post).
- 3 pieces of kiaat 260 x 70 x 30 mm (10¼ x 2¾ x 1¼ in) (for the legs).
- 1 piece of oak 375 x 375 x 22 mm (14¾ x 14¾ x ⅞ in) (for the top). You may have to join one or two boards to achieve this size (see biscuit jointing or dowel jointing, pages 90–91).
- 1 piece of kiaat 120 x 120 x 17 mm (4¾ x 4¾ x ⅝ in) (for the securing plate).
- 1 length of 10 mm (⅜ in) dowel rod.
- 3 No. 8, 60 mm (2¼ in) steel countersunk screws.
- 3 No. 8, 40 mm (1⅝ in) steel countersunk screws.
- 4 No. 8, 25 mm (1 in) steel countersunk screws.
- 1 No. 6, 50 mm (2 in) steel countersunk screws.

- Bench with bench vice
- Lathe
- Carpenter's pencil
- Nail punch (nail set)
- Claw hammer
- Electric drill and drill bits (including countersunk bits)
- Jack plane
- Protective goggles
- Callipers
- Retractable steel tape measure
- Set of lathe chisels
- Steel rule or combination square
- Sandpaper (from coarse to fine)
- Screwdriver
- Tenon saw (back saw)
- Coping saw or hand-held jigsaw
- Rasps or files
- Belt sander
- G-clamps (C-clamps)
- Gouge
- Router
- Spirit level (mason's level)
- White wood glue
- Polyurethane finish

STAGE 1 – TURNING THE CENTRE POST

1 Secure the wood in the bench vice in a vertical position and draw in diagonal lines with a combination square or steel rule in order to establish the centre point.

2 Use a nail punch to make an indentation at the centre point. This will accommodate the back centre pin.

3 Repeat steps 1 and 2 at the other end of the post, then drill a hole in this end only. The hole should be 5 mm (³⁄₁₆ in) deep and at the same diameter as the driving centre pin.

4 Secure the wood in the bench vice in a horizontal position and plane off all four sharp edges and corners along the entire length of the post.

5 Place the wood on the lathe with the drilled hole end on the driving centre. Bolt the tailstock of the back centre firmly in place.

6 Set the tool rest about 5 mm (³⁄₁₆ in) from the wood and about 5 mm (³⁄₁₆ in) below the centre before switching on the lathe.

7 Turn the wood by hand to ensure that it turns freely without touching the tool rest. (This 'hand-turning' exercise should be done whenever the tool support is moved to a new position.)

8 Check that all locking nuts are tight and put on your protective goggles.

9 Stand to the side of the lathe and turn it on. If the wood turns without too much vibration, you are ready to commence turning.

10 Following steps from 7 to 10 from the 'experimenting' section on page 97, turn a cylinder of 65 mm (2½ in) in diameter along the entire length of the post.

11 With the lathe stopped, lay the steel tape on the cylinder and make a pencil mark at 25 mm (1 in) from the left-hand end. Resting the pencil on the tool rest, turn the lathe by hand so that the mark is drawn all the way around the cylinder. The purpose of this is that the mark becomes a continuous line when the wood on the lathe is spinning.

12 First using a round nose lathe chisel and then a narrow square end chisel, turn the wood to the left of this mark down to a cylinder of 25 mm (1 in). This will provide the end support for the post.

13 Switch off the lathe and place the tape on the cylinder at the step you've just created. Make pencil marks on the cylinder at the following distances: 35 mm (1⅜ in), 160 mm (6¼ in) and 210 mm (8¼ in). Turn the lathe by hand so that these marks are drawn right around the cylinder.

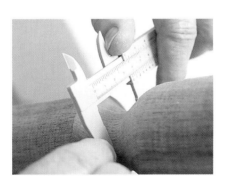

14 Use a round nose chisel to turn a groove down to a diameter of 35 mm (1⅜ in) between the 160 mm (6¼ in) and 210 mm (8¼ in) marks. Make sure that the left-hand side of the curve is concave and the right is convex. Check the diameter with callipers.

15 Repeat step 13, but this time mark points at 420 mm (16½ in) and at 450 mm (18 in). Draw these lines all the way around the cylinder.

16 From the 210 mm (8¼ in) mark to the 420 mm (16½ in) mark, taper the cylinder down to a diameter of 40 mm (1⅝ in), making sure that the taper is slightly convex.

17 To the right of the 450 mm (18 in) mark, turn the end post down to 25 mm (1 in) in diameter, as per step 12.

18 Repeat step 13, making three new marks, at 130 mm (5¼ in), 140 mm (5½ in) and 150 mm (6 in). Using a narrow round nose chisel, turn in a uniform 3 mm (⅛ in) deep groove at each of these marks.

19a From the 35 mm (1⅜ in) mark, turn the left-hand end to a concave taper, ending just short of the support post. Do not go down to a diameter of less than 20 mm (¾ in) otherwise there is the dangerous possibility of this weak point breaking and the wood flying off the lathe. If there is any sign of weakness in the wood at this point, the taper should be finished off by hand at the end of the process, when the wood has been removed from the lathe.

19b Use a narrow square end chisel to turn in the decorative indentations on the taper, as shown in the photograph above.

20 Remove the tool rest from the lathe and, with the wood still turning, use reducing grades of abrasive paper to sand the wood down to a smooth and fine finish.

21 Remove the wood from the lathe and cut off the end support posts.

22 Finish off the tapered end with a bevel-edge chisel, wood file or rasp, and abrasive paper.

STAGE 2 – MAKING THE LEGS

The grain of the wood needs to run with the angle of the leg. If it doesn't, the strength of the legs will be seriously impaired.

1 Make a template for the legs on a rectangle of cardboard measuring 80 x 260 mm (3⅛ x 10¼ in). Use the diagram on page 158 to achieve the suggested shape, although this exact shape is not critical – you can make the legs a little more or a little less curved. Experiment on different pieces of cardboard until you achieve a shape with which you are happy. When you are satisfied that the shape is as you want it, cut it out.

2 Use the template to mark out the legs on all three 260 x 70 x 30 mm (10¼ x 2¾ x 1¼ in) pieces of kiaat.

3 Using a coping saw or electric jigsaw, separately cut out all three legs.

4 Clamp the three legs together and, using rasps and files or the front roller of a belt sander, neaten the shape of the legs so that all three pieces are identical.

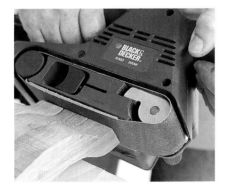

5 With the legs still clamped together, finish all ends to 90° with the surface.

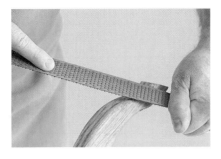

6 Separate the three pieces and use a router, rasps or files to round off the edges (do not round off the ends that will touch the floor or will be joined to the centre post). Finish off with sandpaper.

7 Clamp the legs together again and, using a gouge or the front roller of a belt sander, shape the concave where the legs will join the centre post. This is done by taking out a little bit of wood at a time and then trying the leg against the post until the leg is exactly parallel to the centre post.

8 Drill the screw holes in the legs as shown above.

9 Use the flexible blade of a retractable tape to mark exactly one-third and two-thirds the circumference on the centre post. Extend these marks down the length of this section of post.

10 Test-screw the legs onto the base of the post, and when you are satisfied with their position, glue and screw them in place.

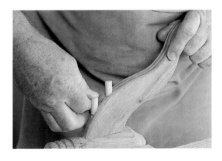

11 Glue a piece of dowel rod into each screw hole, leaving a few millimetres (about ¼ in) exposed to be trimmed off and sanded flush with the surface when the glue is dry.

STAGE 3 – MAKING THE TOP

1 On the chosen underside of the 375 x 375 x 22 mm (14¾ x 14¾ x ⅞ in) piece of oak, lightly draw in the diagonals to establish the centre point.

2 A normal compass will probably be too small to cope with the required diameter, so make your own using a narrow piece of hardboard with a panel pin driven through one end (the point should just protrude from the underside) and another panel pin driven through in the same fashion exactly 185 mm (7¼ in) from the first. Use this inexpensive yet extremely effective compass to 'scratch in' the radius of 185 mm (7¼ in) (diameter 370 mm/ 14½ in) on the wood.

3 Use a jigsaw or coping saw to cut out this circle.

4 Neaten the edge with a belt sander or file until the circle is perfect.

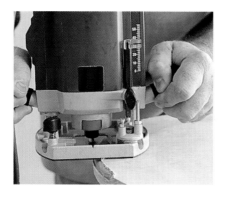

5 Use a router to cut a decorative moulding around the edge.

STAGE 4 – MAKING THE SECURING PLATE

1 Using the 120 x 120 x 17 mm (4¾ x 4¾ x ⅝ in) piece of kiaat, choose which side will be visible (the underside) and use a plane to chamfer the edges.

2 Using a square or steel rule, draw diagonal lines to establish the centre point on the opposite side of the chamfers.

3 Drill a hole through the centre point to accommodate a suitably large screw, which will secure this plate to the centre post. Countersink this hole on the same side as the chamfers.

4 Drill a hole 70 mm (2¾ in) from the centre hole on each of the diagonals. These holes should be countersunk and suitable for No. 8, 25 mm (1 in) steel countersunk screws. Countersink these holes on the same side as the chamfers.

5a Test-screw (without glue) the securing plate to the top and in the centre of the centre post, then screw this section to the centre of the top piece. The pencilled diagonals on the underside of the top should still be visible, so centring should be quite easy.

5b Sand off these pencil marks when you are satisfied that the securing plate is in the correct position.

6 Repeat steps 5a and 5b, but this time apply glue.

7 Sand every part of the table to a fine, smooth finish.

8 Before applying the finish, stand the table on a flat surface and use a spirit level to double-check that the top piece is level.

If the top is not level, small amounts can be trimmed from the bottom of the feet as necessary until the level has been achieved.

9 Apply three coats of polyurethane varnish (see page 105).

Leave each coat to dry completely (allow at least 24 hours' drying time) before sanding it with a fine abrasive paper (about 800 grit), and then apply the next coat. Do not sand the final coat.

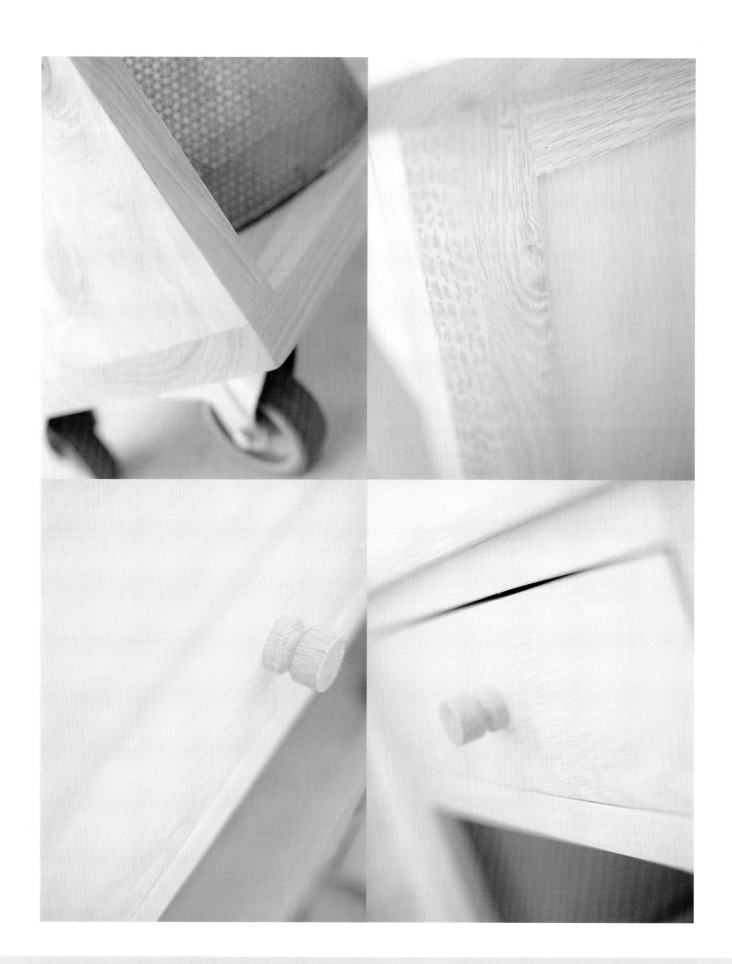

All the wood used for this project is poplar, with the exception of the 6 mm (¼ in) plywood panelling, but other light-coloured hardwoods, such as oak or beech, or even a softwood such as pine, will suffice.

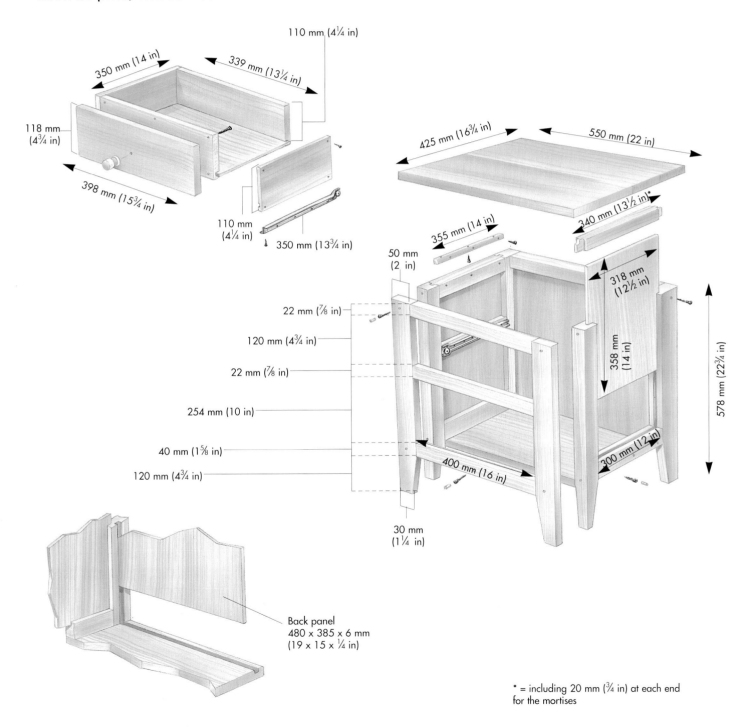

110 mm (4¼ in)

350 mm (14 in)

339 mm (13¼ in)

118 mm (4¾ in)

398 mm (15¾ in)

110 mm (4¼ in)

350 mm (13¾ in)

425 mm (16¾ in)

550 mm (22 in)

340 mm (13½ in)*

355 mm (14 in)

318 mm (12½ in)

50 mm (2 in)

22 mm (⅞ in)

120 mm (4¾ in)

22 mm (⅞ in)

358 mm (14 in)

578 mm (22¾ in)

254 mm (10 in)

40 mm (1⅝ in)

120 mm (4¾ in)

400 mm (16 in)

300 mm (12 in)

30 mm (1¼ in)

Back panel
480 x 385 x 6 mm
(19 x 15 x ¼ in)

* = including 20 mm (¾ in) at each end for the mortises

Top

- 1 piece of poplar 550 x 425 x 22 mm (22 x 16¾ x ⅞ in) thick. You will probably need to biscuit joint (see page 91) or dowel joint (see page 90) several boards to achieve this width.

Bottom shelf

- 1 piece of poplar 456 x 385 x 22 mm (18 x 15 x ⅞ in) thick. As for the top of the cabinet, you may need to join several boards to achieve this width.

Front frame

- Uprights: 2 pieces of poplar 578 x 50 x 22 mm (22¾ x 2 x ⅞ in) thick.
- Top and centre rails: 2 pieces of poplar 440 x 30 x 22 mm (17¼ x 1¼ x ⅞ in) thick.
- Bottom rail: 1 piece of poplar 440 x 40 x 22 mm (17¼ x 1⅝ x ⅞ in) thick.

Side frames

- Back legs: 2 pieces of poplar 578 x 30 x 22 mm (22¾ x 1¼ x ⅞ in) thick.
- Front legs: 2 pieces of poplar 578 x 50 x 22 mm (22¾ x 2 x ⅞ in) thick.
- Top rails: 2 pieces of poplar 340 x 50 x 22 mm (13½ x 2 x ⅞ in) thick.
- Bottom rails: 2 pieces of poplar 340 x 70 x 22 mm (13½ x 2¾ x ⅞ in) thick.
- Panels: 2 pieces of 6 mm (¼ in) plywood (preferably with an oak veneer) 358 x 318 mm (14 x 12½ in).
- Drawer runner supports: 2 pieces of poplar 300 x 30 x 20 mm (12 x 1¼ x ⅞ in) thick.
- 2 side cleats: 355 x 22 x 22 mm (14 x ⅞ x ⅞ in) thick.
- 1 back cleat: 410 x 22 x 22 mm (16 x ⅞ x ⅞ in) thick.

Back

- Top rail: 1 piece of poplar 460 x 50 x 22 mm (18 x 2 x ⅞ in) thick.
- Panel: 1 piece of 6 mm (¼ in) plywood (preferably with an oak veneer) 480 x 385 mm (19 x 15 in).

Drawer

- Sides: 2 pieces of poplar 350 x 110 x 18 mm (14 x 4¼ x ¾ in) thick.
- Back: 1 piece of poplar 339 x 110 x 18 mm (13¼ x 4¼ x ¾ in) thick.
- Inside front: 1 piece of poplar 339 x 110 x 18 mm (13¼ x 4¼ x ¾ in) thick.
- Bottom panel: 1 piece of 6 mm (¼ in) plywood 330 x 350 mm (13 x 14 in).
- Front: 1 piece of poplar 398 x 118 x 22 mm thick (15¾ x 4¾ x ⅞ in)
- 1 suitable drawer knob.
- 1 set of drawer runners 350 mm (13¾ in) long.

- 31 No. 8, 30 mm (1¼ in) steel countersunk screws.
- 4 No. 10, 15 mm (⅝ in) steel countersunk screws.

- Bench with bench vice
- Carpenter's pencil
- Tenon saw (back saw)
- Router
- Screwdriver
- White wood glue
- Wood filler
- Sandpaper (coarse to fine)
- Lime wash
- Polyurethane varnish

STAGE 1 – MAKING UP THE UNIT

They say that a picture is worth a thousand words – keep referring to the photographs and the diagrams to make sure that the instructions are clear.

1 Mark out and cut the taper on the feet of the uprights (there should be six).

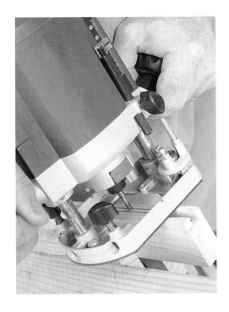

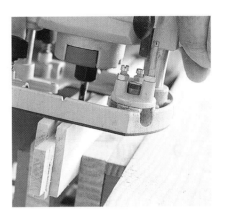

2 Starting 10 mm (⅜ in) from the outside face of the top and bottom side rails and the back top rail, use a router to cut grooves 6 mm (¼ in) wide and 10 mm (⅜ in) deep. These grooves will accommodate the side and back panels.

4 Fit the front frame together dry (without glue) to ensure that it is accurate and, when satisfied, glue it together.

6 Fit a guide to the router and cut grooves 6 mm (¼ in) wide and 10 mm (⅜ in) deep in the bottom shelf, sides and the back rail to accommodate the backing ply.

7 Assemble the sides to the bottom shelf, insert the backing ply and screw the top rail into place.

3 Cut the haunched mortise and tenon joints (see pages 76–77) for the front frame.

5 Fit the side frames together dry (and with the panels in place) to ensure that they fit properly and, when satisfied, glue up the side frames.

8 Screw the front frame into position on the side frames.

9 Sand the box unit.

10 Put on the top by screwing vertically (but at an angle) through the front and side cleats.

STAGE 2 – ASSEMBLING THE DRAWER

1 Use the router to cut grooves, 6 mm (¼ in) wide and 10 mm (⅜ in) deep, in the sides, the inside front and the back to accommodate the plywood panel for the drawer bottom. (Refer to the diagram detail on page 121.)

2 Assemble the drawer, making sure that the panel fits into the groove of all four pieces of the box construction.

3 Screw the drawer runners into position, insert the drawer and slide it back and forth to check that it runs smoothly.

4 Line up the front face of the drawer and screw this piece onto the drawer from the inside to the drawer box.

STAGE 3 – FINISHING OFF

1 Sand the whole cabinet.

2 Fill any holes or small gaps with a matching wood filler, then sand these fillings flat when dry.

3 Apply lime wash (see page 109) and, when dry, seal the unit with polyurethane varnish (see page 105).

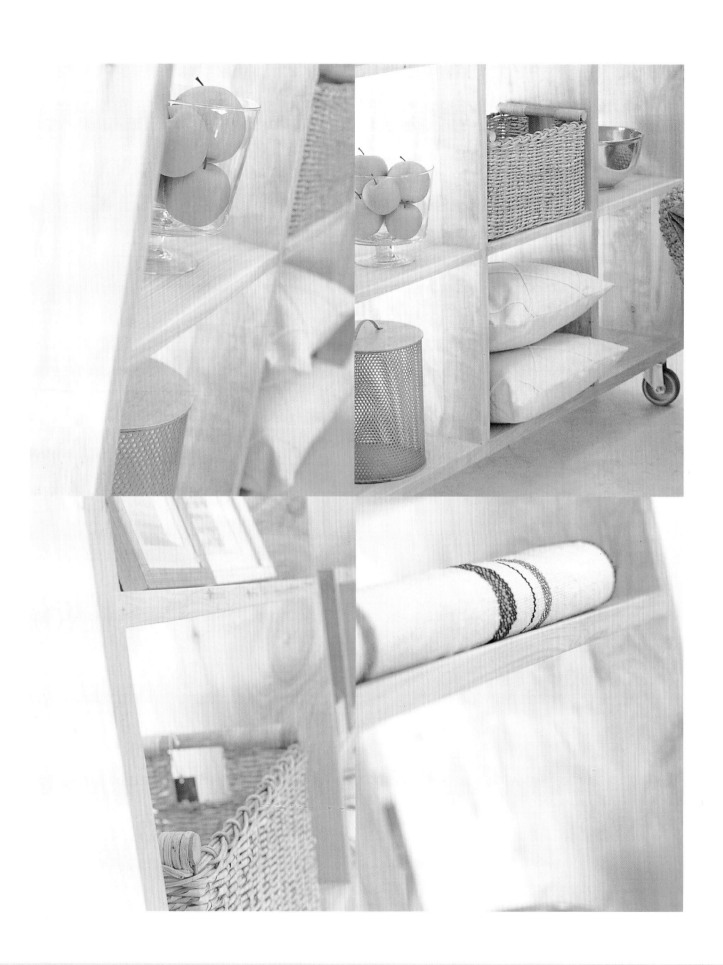

PROJECT THREE: ROOM DIVIDER

Before trying this particular unit, it is worth considering whether these internal shelving arrangements are going to suit your purposes. For example, a television or video recorder may fit better if the measurements are different. It is a relatively simple process to copy the above plan and then make your personal changes, as the assembly method described below will be the same for both. The wood used in this project is poplar, but other hardwoods such as oak or mahogany are also suitable.

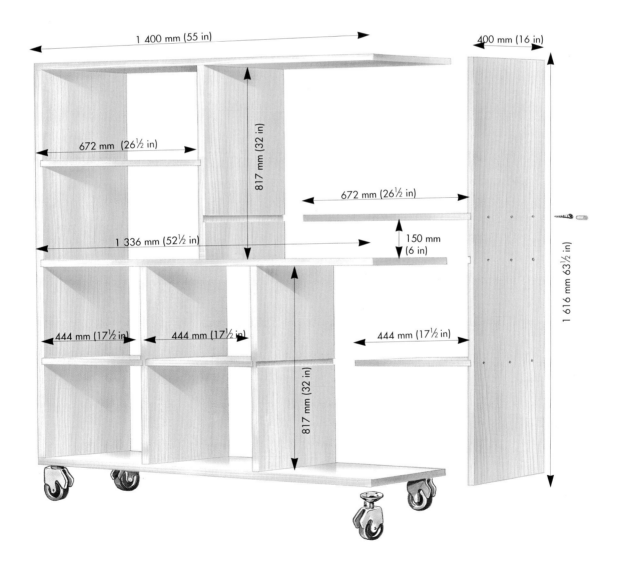

- Two thicknesses of board are required for this job: 32 mm (1¼ in) for the four sides of the frame and the vertical sections; and 22 mm (⅞ in) for the horizontal sections, with the exception of the top and bottom pieces.

- All boards must be finished to 400 mm (16 in) wide, which will probably mean biscuit jointing (see page 91) or dowel jointing (see page 90) several boards to achieve this width.

32 mm (1¼ in) thick boards

- 2 pieces of poplar 1 616 mm (63½ in) long (for the right and left uprights).
- 3 pieces of poplar 817 mm (32 in) long (for the upright dividers).
- 2 pieces of poplar 1 400 mm (55 in) long (for the top and bottom).

22 mm (⅞ in) thick boards

- 2 pieces of poplar 672 mm (26½ in) long (for the shelves of the top half).
- 3 pieces of poplar 444 mm (17½ in) long (for the shelves of the lower half).
- 1 piece of poplar 1 336 mm (52½ in) long (for the middle shelf, running from side to side).

- 54 No. 8, 50 mm (2 in) steel countersunk screws.
- 1 length of 10 mm (⅜ in) dowel rod.
- 4 castors with screws (optional).

- Bench with bench vice
- Carpenter's pencil
- Tenon saw (back saw)
- Large steel square
- Bradawl
- Router
- G-clamps (C-clamps)
- Bevel-edge (paring) chisel
- Carpenter's wooden mallet
- White wood glue
- Wood filler
- Polyurethane varnish

HELPFUL HINT

It is a good idea to write lightly on each piece of wood as it is cut to size, to identify it throughout the project, for example: 'top inside front' or 'left lower shelf front'. These notations will disappear in the final sanding.

1 Cut all boards to the correct dimensions and lightly write a description on each board as per the hint above.

2a You will notice from the diagram that all the 32 mm (1¼ in) boards for the uprights should be dowel jointed (see pages 85–86).

2b All the 22 mm (⅞ in) boards for the shelves will be held in position by through housing joints (see pages 86–87). This means that only the uprights will have housing slots cut into them.

3 Mark out all the boards according to the diagram and use a large steel square to continue the pencil lines across the relevant surfaces.

4 Check that all lines indicating where the housing slots are to be cut (on the uprights) are exactly the same as the thickness of the shelves they will receive.

5 On the uprights only, score the pencil lines across the surfaces with a bradawl.

6 Draw in hatching lines to indicate the area in the slots which needs to be cut out with a router.

7 When you are positive that all of these markings are accurate, use a router set to 10 mm (⅜ in) deep to cut the housing slots. (Clamping a guide strip in place will help to get an accurate, straight cut.)

8 Without using glue, butt and screw the top and bottom sections to the left and right uprights to form the outer frame. This is best achieved by laying the frame on the floor.

9 Insert the middle shelf (without glue) and make any adjustments as you go.

10 Without using glue, butt and screw the centre top upright and the two lower uprights into position, making any minor adjustments as you go.

16 Fill the screw head holes in the outer frame, either with dowel plugs or wood filler, to match the colour of the wood.

17 Fill any gaps with wood filler and sand flush with the surface when dry.

18 Sand the entire unit to a smooth, fine finish.

19 Seal the room divider with three coats of polyurethane varnish (see page 105), allowing each coat to dry for 24 hours before lightly sanding the unit and applying the next coat.

11 Insert all the shelves (also without glue), making any adjustments to the slots as you go.

12 When you are satisfied that everything fits together accurately, disassemble the whole unit.

13 Repeat step 8, but this time apply white wood glue before assembling the top and bottom sections and the left and right uprights to form the outer frame. Wipe away any excess glue squeezed out of the joints.

14 When the outer frame is dry, glue the uprights into position and use a mallet to ensure that they are exactly flush with the frame. Leave the glue to dry.

15 After the uprights are dry, glue all the shelves into position in the same way as step 14.

20 If you want the unit to be mobile, secure a sturdy castor on each corner (similar to the one shown in the photograph). Make sure that the castors are set sufficiently under the unit to prevent toe-stubbing!

PROJECT FOUR: DINING TABLE

This table is made entirely from oak, but any durable hardwood can be used in its place.

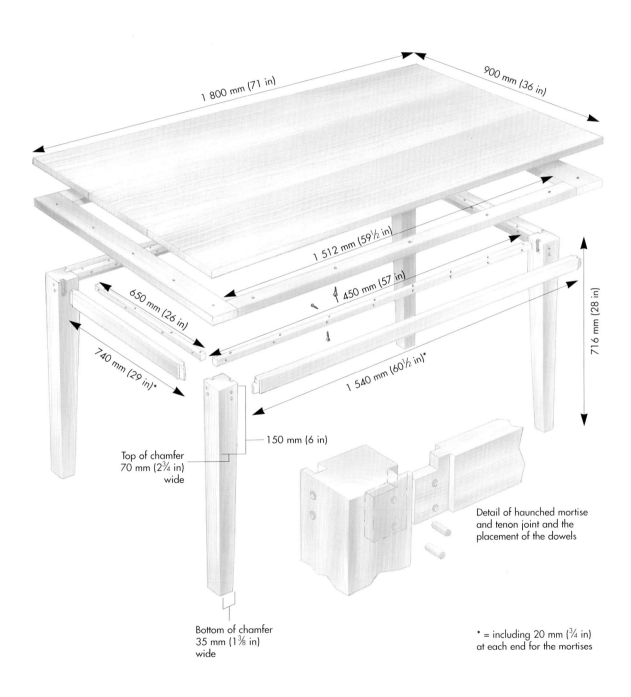

1 800 mm (71 in)

900 mm (36 in)

1 512 mm (59½ in)

450 mm (57 in)

650 mm (26 in)

740 mm (29 in)*

1 540 mm (60½ in)*

716 mm (28 in)

150 mm (6 in)

Top of chamfer
70 mm (2¾ in)
wide

Bottom of chamfer
35 mm (1⅜ in)
wide

Detail of haunched mortise
and tenon joint and the
placement of the dowels

* = including 20 mm (¾ in)
at each end for the mortises

- Top: 1 piece of oak 2 100 x 900 x 22 mm (82¾ x 36 x ⅞ in) thick. This will need to be made up from several boards – biscuit jointing (see page 91) is the most suitable method, but dowel jointing (see page 90) will suffice.
- Legs: 4 pieces of oak 716 x 70 x 70 mm (28 x 2¾ x 2¾ in) thick.
- Side of top: 2 pieces of oak 1 512 x 90 x 22 mm (59½ x 3½ x ⅞ in) thick.
- End stretchers: 2 pieces of oak 740 x 120 x 22 mm (29 in x 4¾ x ⅞ in) thick.
- Side stretchers: 2 pieces of oak 1 540 x 120 x 22 mm (60½ x 4¾ x ⅞ in) thick.
- Cleats (to secure the top to the base): 2 cleats 650 x 22 x 22 mm (26 x ⅞ x ⅞ in) thick; 2 cleats 1 450 x 22 x 22 mm (57 x ⅞ x ⅞ in) thick.
- 1 length of 10 mm (⅜ in) dowel rod.
- 44 No. 8, 45 mm (1¾ in) steel countersunk screws.

- Bench with bench vice
- Carpenter's pencil
- Marking gauge
- Steel rule
- Try square
- Tenon saw (back saw)
- Jack plane
- Mortise gauge
- Mortise or firmer (framing) chisel
- Carpenter's wooden mallet
- Sandpaper (coarse to fine)
- Screwdriver
- Retractable steel tape measure
- Sash cramps (bar clamps)
- White wood glue
- Wood filler
- Polyurethane varnish

3 Mark out the mortises (see pages 76–77) on each leg and, before chopping them out, make sure that the chamfers will be on the inside surfaces when the joints are fitted.

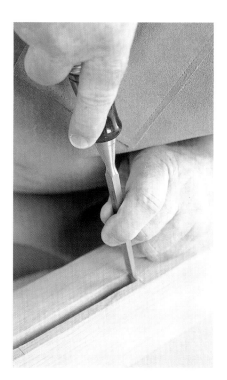

1 Secure each leg piece in the bench vice and mark out the two inside surfaces for the chamfer.

2 Using a tenon saw, cut these chamfers to approximately 2 mm (⅟₁₆ in) from the marked line, and then use a jack plane to plane the legs down to the line.

4 Chop out the mortises with a mortise or firmer chisel.

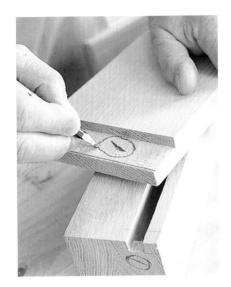

5 Mark out and cut the tenons on the ends of all four stretchers but, as each tenon is cut, fit it into one of the mortises, make any necessary adjustments and then number each joint in pencil so that it's clear which pieces belong together when the table frame is assembled.

6 Fit the table frame together dry (without glue) to ensure that the joints fit properly, and check that the frame is square.

7 When satisfied that the frame fits together well, glue it up and secure it with sash cramps. When the glue has set, add the dowels to strengthen the joints. The dowels are glued and hammered into holes drilled through the outer corners of the legs and through the mortise and tenon joints (see the detail diagram on page 133). Care should be taken not to drill all the way through to the inside surface of the leg.

8 Measure, mark and then cut 150 mm (6 in) off each end of the table top section.

9 Glue and screw the ends underneath the same ends from which they have been cut, to give the impression of a solid 44 mm (1¾ in) thick top.

13 Fit cleats to the base and secure the top onto the base with screws.

10 Take the two side top pieces and carefully fit them dry before gluing and screwing them into position. The sides must be fitted under the top in the same way as the ends.

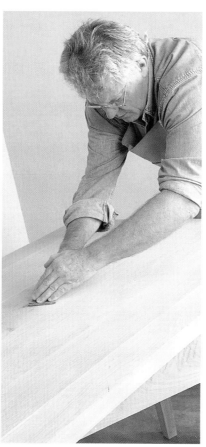

11 Fill all screw holes and any gaps with matching wood filler.

12 Completely sand down the top and base.

14 Seal the table with three coats of polyurethane varnish (see page 105), allowing each coat to dry for 24 hours before lightly sanding the whole table and applying the next coat.

138 the woodworker's handbook

PROJECT FIVE: DINING CHAIR

This chair is also made entirely from oak to match the dining table, but any suitable hardwood can be used in its place.

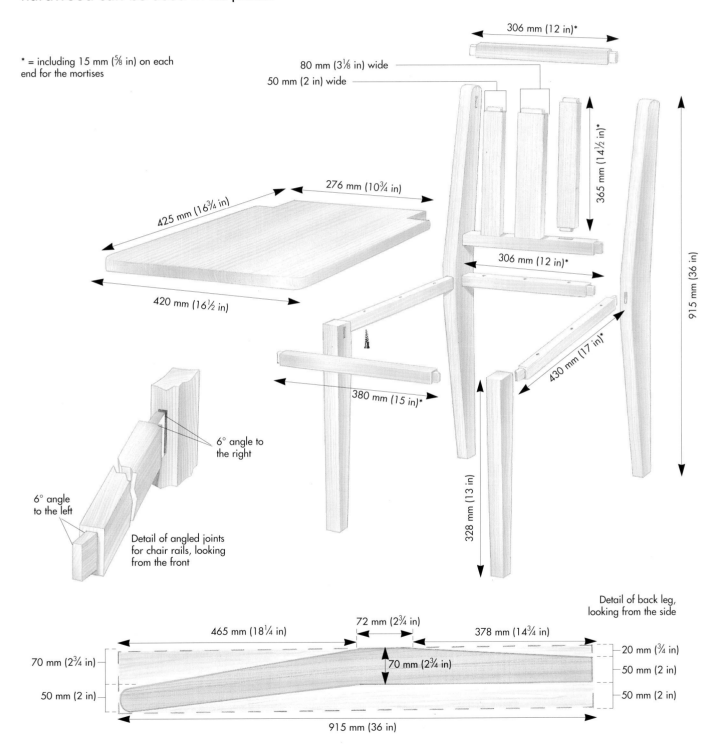

* = including 15 mm (⁵⁄₈ in) on each end for the mortises

306 mm (12 in)*

80 mm (3⅛ in) wide
50 mm (2 in) wide

365 mm (14½ in)*

276 mm (10¾ in)

425 mm (16¾ in)

420 mm (16½ in)

306 mm (12 in)*

915 mm (36 in)

430 mm (17 in)*

380 mm (15 in)*

328 mm (13 in)

6° angle to the right

6° angle to the left

Detail of angled joints for chair rails, looking from the front

Detail of back leg, looking from the side

465 mm (18¼ in)

72 mm (2¾ in)

378 mm (14¾ in)

70 mm (2¾ in)

70 mm (2¾ in)

20 mm (¾ in)

50 mm (2 in)

50 mm (2 in)

50 mm (2 in)

915 mm (36 in)

- Seat: 1 piece of oak 425 x 420 x 22 mm (16¾ x 16½ x ⅞ in) thick.
- Back legs: 2 pieces of oak 915 x 120 x 32 mm (36 x 4¾ x 1¼ in) thick.
- Front legs: 2 pieces of oak 328 x 70 x 70 mm (13 x 2¾ x 2¾ in) thick.
- Seat rails, sides (stretchers): 2 pieces of oak 430 x 50 x 22 mm (17 x 2 x ⅞ in) thick.
- Seat rail, front (stretcher): 1 piece of oak 380 x 50 x 22 mm (15 x 2 x ⅞ in) thick.
- Seat rail, back (stretcher): 1 piece of oak 306 x 50 x 22 mm (12 x 2 x ⅞ in) thick.
- Chair back, top and bottom rail: 2 pieces of oak 306 x 50 x 22 mm (12 x 2 x ⅞ in) thick.
- Chair back, vertical centre rail: 1 piece of oak 365 x 80 x 22 mm (14½ x 3⅛ x ⅞ in) thick.
- Chair back, vertical outside rails: 2 pieces of oak 365 x 50 x 22 mm (14½ x 2 x ⅞ in) thick.
- 12 No. 8, 65 mm (2½ in) steel countersunk screws.

- Bench with bench vice
- Carpenter's pencil
- Steel rule
- Retractable steel tape measure
- Hand-held jigsaw
- Jack plane
- Rasp
- Mortise gauge
- Mortise or firmer (framing) chisel
- Carpenter's wooden mallet
- Crosscut saw
- Tenon saw (back saw)
- Adjustable bevel (sliding T-bevel)
- Sandpaper (coarse to fine)
- Screwdriver
- White wood glue
- Wood filler
- Polyurethane varnish

3 Mark out, cut and then shape the tapers on the front legs.

4 Mark out the mortises (see pages 76–77) in the front and back legs as per the diagram, then chop these out with a mortise or firmer chisel.

5 Mark out and then cut the tenons on the front and back stretchers according to the diagram.

1 Mark out the back legs as per the diagram on page 139 and cut them out with a jigsaw.

2 Neaten and finish off the back legs using a jack plane and a rasp.

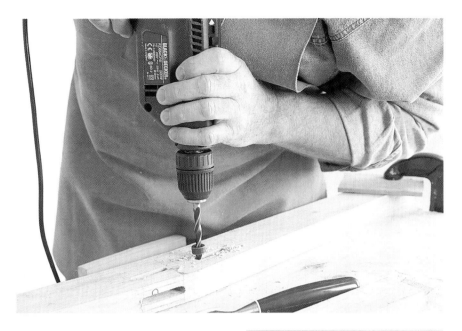

6 Mark out and cut the tenons on the side stretchers according to the diagram. You will notice from this diagram that the tenons are angled at 6°. Make sure that when the angled tenons are cut on these stretchers there is one for each side – don't cut them both the same!

8 Before gluing the frame together, mark and chop out the mortise holes on the top and bottom rails for the back of the chair, according to the diagram.

7 Fit the legs and stretchers together dry (without glue) to check that all the joints fit properly and make any necessary adjustments.

9 Mark out and cut the tenons for the top and bottom rails of the back of the chair.

10 Put these joints together dry (without glue) to ensure a good fit (it helps to number corresponding sections of the joints to avoid confusion when gluing up).

16 Glue the front stretcher into the front legs and leave it to dry.

17 Glue the side rails into the front and back sections so that the whole chair frame is now assembled.

11 Mark and chop out the mortise holes for the vertical rails on the back top and bottom rail.

12 Mark and cut the tenons in the vertical rails.

13 Put these joints together dry to ensure a good fit (number corresponding sections of the joints to avoid confusion when gluing up).

14 Put the whole frame together dry to ensure that it fits properly.

15 Glue up the back section of the chair and allow it to dry.

18 Glue and screw the seat into position through the side rails.

19 Fill all screw holes and any gaps with a matching wood filler.

20 Sand down the whole chair, then seal it with three coats of polyurethane varnish (see page 105), allowing each coat to dry for 24 hours before lightly sanding the whole chair and applying the next coat.

repairs and restoration

There are a number of reasons why it will be necessary to repair wooden furniture from time to time. Everyday use results in wear and tear, which eventually causes damage. And, unlike other materials, wood is a living substance which, although technically dead when made into furniture, still retains some of the characteristics of life – it will absorb moisture and expand, or dry out in hot climates and contract or split, necessitating repairs.

There are also the problems of glue failure as older wood glues, such as bone glues (literally made by boiling bones and animal hooves into a glutinous, foul-smelling mess), become brittle with age and may cause joints to fail.

Unfortunately, almost everybody has 'had a go' at fixing their own damaged furniture, attempting to join wood with unsuitable glues or even over-sized nails, which can lead to greater problems than the original damage. But, in spite of this sort of experience, successful repairs are not that difficult to achieve if you apply a little common sense and a few learned skills.

The only additional equipment needed will be about three metres (10 ft) of sash cord or similar rope, white water-based (PVA) white wood glue and a craft knife.

Cord and toggle
Long sash cramps are very expensive, and most woodworkers would not have more than two or three in their workshop. When gluing up complex pieces of furniture, such as a chair, it often happens that there are not enough sash cramps to hold the project in position, or the cramps are simply too tricky to apply. When this occurs, an alternative method of applying pressure is needed.

This is where the 'cord and toggle' method comes into its own. It consists of a length of strong cord (skipping rope, sash cord or nylon cord), which is tied once around the joint. A small slat of wood or something similar is then inserted between the sections of cord and is turned to make the cord tighter. When the pressure is sufficient, the toggle is twisted to rest against a section of the structure in order to prevent the cord unwinding (see photograph on page 42). Make sure that there is some packing, such as mutton cloth, between the cord and the wood to prevent marking the surface.

Broken rails

This is one of the most common repair jobs that needs to be done, and there are two important aspects to remember when approaching a repair of this nature.

First, if the break is clean there is a good chance of achieving an almost perfect repair as, with the application of some white wood glue, the fibres of the two broken pieces should fit very well together, and the combined surface area of all the broken fibres being glued together will make for a strong and satisfactory repair.

Second, for the join to fit properly, pressure has to be applied so that the glue will set under pressure and in the correct position. A sash cramp should be used for most repairs, but make sure that the pressure is applied directly along the natural line of the wood. There are six basic steps involved in this kind of repair.

1 Check the broken ends to ensure that they are clean.

2 Push the rail together dry (without glue) to make sure you know which way round it goes and that the ends marry properly.

3 Use a small paintbrush to apply white wood glue onto each of the broken ends, ensuring that the entire inside surface area of the break has a coating of glue.

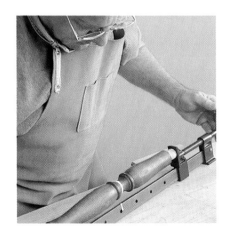

4 Join the two pieces, checking that they match exactly, and apply pressure with the sash cramp.

5 Wipe away excess glue with a damp, soft cloth.

6 Allow the joint to set – leave it for 24 hours to ensure a complete setting.

Sometimes a rail of a chair can fracture while the end joints remain intact. In this case, fix one of the chair legs in a bench vice and move the fracture apart just enough to paint both broken ends with wood glue. A sash cramp can then be set on the outside of the structure and pressure applied before wiping away the surplus glue that has been squeezed out of the joint.

Repairing a thin rail

When a thin rail is fractured, there is often not much surface area that can be glued together to make the joint strong again. In this instance, it is a good idea to strengthen the joint by inserting a dowel rod into it.

2 Push the rail together dry (without glue) to make sure that the ends marry properly.

3 Use a small paintbrush to apply white wood glue onto each of the broken ends, ensuring that the entire inside surface area of the break has a coating of glue.

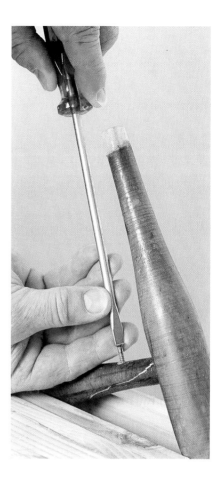

Although it can be quite tricky to drill the holes for the dowel rod exactly in the centre of the rail, it is a worthwhile exercise, as the resulting joint will hold better than glue.

Rails split along the grain

Due to aging or too much lateral pressure, a rail can split along the grain, which itself may not be parallel to the sides of the wood.

To repair this type of damage, do the following:

1 Check the broken ends to ensure that they are clean.

4 Clamp up the join with a G-clamp, placing a piece of wax paper between the protective block on the clamp's jaws and the wood that is being repaired. If any excess glue seeps out of the join, the wax paper will prevent the clamp from getting stuck to the wood.

5 Use a soft, damp cloth to wipe away excess glue and leave the joint to set for 24 hours.

6a This joint can be further strengthened by inserting appropriately sized screws, preferably before the glue has set.

6b Sometimes, however, due to restricted access between the G-clamps, this will have to be done after the joint has set. Once the screws are in place, fill the indentations left by the screw heads with wood filler and sand this flush with the surrounding surface when it is dry.

Splits or fractures to very thin rails

Thin rails or dowels (up to about 12 mm/½ in in diameter) are not particularly strong and tend to fracture or split if too much pressure is applied.

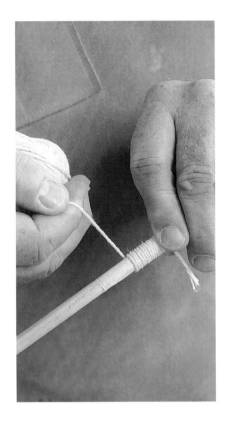

WOBBLY JOINTS

It is almost inevitable that the joints of wooden furniture will begin to move slightly or 'wobble' through regular use. This occurs most frequently with mortise and tenon joints in tables and chairs, and corner joints, such as dovetail joints, in drawers and cabinets.

1 If the split or fracture extends along most of the length of the dowel, paint both surfaces with wood glue, wrap a piece of wax paper around the joint and then tightly coil string around the wax paper. If the joint is unwrapped after about three hours, it will be easy to remove the semi-solid white glue from the surface, while the joint will be firm enough to continue the setting process on its own.

2 If the split in the rail is quite short, paint the fractured ends with white wood glue, wrap the joint in wax paper and then bind the join with electrical insulating tape. The tape will provide lateral support while the glue is setting. After a few hours, remove the insulating tape and peel off the glue on the outside of the joint.

Repairing mortise and tenon joints

1 Carefully take the joint apart, first checking whether it was originally fixed with dowels, screws or nails. If there is no evidence of these, then a few gentle taps with the broad surface of a mallet may bring the joint apart without too much effort.

If the joint has been secured with dowels, drill out the dowel with a drill bit that is the same diameter as the dowel. Caution should be exercised when drilling out a dowel because you will be drilling into the end grain, which may cause the drill bit to wander and damage the surrounding wood. For this reason, a flat bit is more suitable than a standard twist bit. Another reason to be cautious is that what may appear to be a dowel could be wood filler or a short dowel plug on top of a screw head.

2 Number the parts of the joint with a pencil (ensuring that the markings will not be visible when the joint is reconstructed), so that you can easily determine which parts go together.

3 Remove all traces of old glue so that the surfaces to be rejoined are clean down to the bare wood. If you accidentally chip out bits of wood as you remove the glue, resulting in a loose-fitting joint, the joint can be glued up with epoxy (see page 73) as this will become solid and strong and will fill any gaps.

4 When glued, clamp up the joint, remembering to place a piece of wax paper between the clamp's protective blocks and the wood.

5 Use a soft, damp cloth to remove excess glue squeezed out of the joint, and leave it to set for 24 hours.

Sometimes when a mortise and tenon joint is broken, damage may occur to the tenon as a result of an old dowel still being in place. Possibly the best solution here is to drill out the old dowel. Ensure that there is no wood remaining inside the mortise, and then cut away about one-third of the old tenon. A new sliver of wood (the same size as the cut-off section) can then be glued to the old tenon. When the joint is reglued it can also be redoweled, usually through the same hole used for the previous dowel.

When making up a new tenon, the joint's strength can be enhanced by the addition of a haunch.

If the tenon has been completely snapped off at its base, the best solution is to make up a new tenon (see pages 76–77) which can be mortised into the old rail as well as the original mortise.

Repairing dovetail joints
The most common repair involving dovetail joints is when a drawer begins to fall apart. To repair this, do the following:

1 If possible, take the drawer apart completely. Probably the greatest danger when endeavouring to separate reluctant joints is that, because the drawer sides are usually quite thin, damage may occur if they are tackled too vigorously. In order to avoid this, place a long block of scrap wood against the inside of the joint and tap gently on this with a mallet.

Another problem that you may encounter is when the drawer bottom has been nailed to the rear of the drawer. Place a block of scrap wood against the end and the drawer bottom and tap gently with a mallet or hammer until the drawer bottom comes away by about 4 mm (³⁄₁₆ in). If the nails are in good condition and the nail head is broad enough, the nail will be drawn away with the bottom of the drawer. Then all you need to do is tap the drawer bottom back into position, leaving the nail head exposed and making it possible to extract the nail with pincers.

2 Remove all traces of old glue until the surfaces to be rejoined are clean down to the bare wood.

3 Put the drawer together dry (without glue) to check that the joint fits together well.

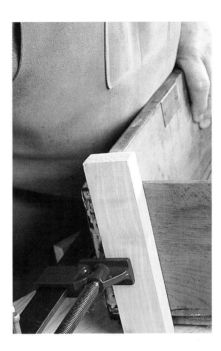

4 Apply wood glue to the parts to be joined and clamp up the joints. If the drawer is quite deep, it will be necessary to distribute the pressure of the sash cramp along the entire width of the joint. This can be achieved by placing a long block of scrap wood between the drawer and the cramp.

5 Use a soft, damp cloth to remove any excess wood glue and leave the joint to set for 24 hours.

The previous examples have described the restoration of the most commonly damaged joints, but whatever the joint, the basic principles remain the same, that of taking the joint to pieces as neatly and with as little damage as possible, cleaning up the joint, and regluing it. Most joints will respond to this kind of restorative process. Some will be easy, some will be tricky, but a little thought and a great deal of initiative will turn these seemingly daunting tasks into challenges resulting in satisfying success!

Stripped screw threads

A common problem in repairing or restoring furniture occurs when a screw has either lost its grip in a piece of wood or has been stripped out by accidental force. Due to the damaged wood in the screw hole, there is no point in replacing the screw. There is, however, another way to repair the damage.

1 Cut a wooden cone roughly the same size as the damaged screw.

2 Coat the cone with wood glue and also squeeze a little glue into the hole that is to receive the cone.

3 Tap the cone into place with a hammer and leave the glue to dry for 24 hours. After it is set, the excess can be trimmed flush with the surface of the surrounding wood and a new lead hole for the screw can be drilled.

DAMAGE TO SURFACES

As furniture is used, and abused, the surfaces of tables and cabinets will become damaged from time to time. Apart from general wear and tear, heavy objects are dropped on them, hot saucepans are placed on them, liquids are spilled on them and scratches just 'happen'!

Some of these problems can be solved by treating the particular area concerned, but on other occasions a complete resurfacing may need to be considered. Let's start with the easier ones.

Dents

If a heavy object is dropped on the surface of wood, the wood fibres become compressed. If the dent is not too deep (less than 2 mm/¹⁄₁₆ in) the compressed grain of the wood can often be restored by putting a few drops of boiling water into the dent. If this is successful, allow the surface to dry thoroughly before applying a finish to the restored area.

If the hot-water method does not work or the dent is too deep, the indentation will need to be filled with wood filler. It's always a good idea to have a number of different colours of commercially produced wood filler in your workshop. If these are all produced by the same manufacturer, different colours can be mixed together to obtain a match with the surrounding wood (see page 103). Keep in mind that the more surface area that the filler can grip, the longer it will stay in the hole. To assist with this, deepen the dent slightly with a bradawl or small chisel (do not make it any wider, only deeper).

It may take a few minutes for the wood to absorb the water and recover its original appearance.

Tightly press wood filler into the indentation until it is slightly proud of the surface, and leave it to dry for 24 hours. When dry, sand the filler flush with the surrounding surface.

Scratches

The severity of the damage will determine the action to be taken. A superficial scratch may damage only the finish and not the wooden surface underneath. If this is the case, lightly rubbing over the surface with very fine steel wool may well be sufficient to remove any visible marks.

If the scratch has penetrated through to the wood but is still quite superficial, the 'boiling water' technique used for dents can sometimes rectify the problem.

If the scratch is fairly deep, about the best you can do, short of resurfacing the entire piece, is to match the wood by mixing wood filler and filling and resealing the scratch mark. This is not the ideal solution as a scratch can be very difficult to disguise, especially if it lies across the grain of the wood. If you are very particular about the appearance of your furniture, it may be as well to consider resurfacing the entire area (see below).

Burns

Modern polyurethane finishes will resist burn damage to the wood, but occasionally a severe burn will penetrate the wood surface underneath. Some small burns, such as cigarette burns, can be treated by scratching away the burned wood with a sharp curved blade. If the burn is superficial, the hot water method used for repairing dents may cause the grain to swell enough for the problem to be solved.

Larger burn marks, such as those caused by the base of a hot saucepan, may cover a fairly wide area, but these also tend to be superficial. In this instance, the surface of the burn and the immediate area surrounding the burn can be removed with a cabinet scraper or an orbital sander. As this will only remove a fraction of the finish and surface, the remaining shallow indentation will be barely noticeable.

It is unusual for a burn of this nature to penetrate very far into the wood, but if this does happen, a complete resurfacing will have to be considered (see below).

Complete resurfacing

1 Check whether the surface of the piece is made of solid wood or if it has a veneer. Because veneer is usually only 1.5 mm (about 1/16 in) thick, great care has to be taken not to sand or scrape through the veneer to the wood underneath. If this happens, it will result in an ugly contrast to the remaining veneer, which will be almost impossible to disguise.

2 Use a cabinet scraper, belt sander or orbital sander to remove the surface finish. Avoid using a plane, as certain finishes will blunt a plane blade very quickly.

3 If the surface is solid wood, use a cabinet scraper, plane or sander to remove just enough of the surface to get down to clean, bare wood.

4 If some deep indentations or scratches still remain, use wood filler to fill these and sand them flush with the surface once dry.

5 When a clean, flat surface has been re-established you may need to apply wood stain before finishing off in order to get as close as possible to the original colour of the wood. Like wood fillers, wood stains come in a large variety of colours and mixing different colours from the same manufacturer will usually result in a close match. It is a good idea to mix a small quantity first and test it out on a scrap piece of wood, then allow it to dry properly before attempting to recolour the entire surface (see page 104).

6 Apply a polyurethane finish rather than any other as this is probably the best and most durable modern finish available (see page 105).

chapter seven

your own designs

One of the great thrills arising from the hobby of woodworking is the construction of projects that have been conceived, designed and built by yourself.

There are a distinct number of stages in the process of conception to completion, but perhaps the most important factor is the ability to visualize the completed project, as this will enable you to successfully work through the stages until you achieve the end result.

The thinking stage can be a great adventure in and of itself. I find the best position for this stage is horizontal, with hands folded on the chest, eyes closed and a pillow under the head – and I'm quite serious about that!

If I allow my mind to wander across a potential project at this conceptual stage, it takes on a real form in my mind: decisions on joints are made; the way parts fit together is visualized and the various steps through the construction process established, from the type of wood used to the final finish. It also depends upon whether you are thinking of building a project just for pure enjoyment, or whether it will fulfil a specific need.

THINKING STAGE

It is advisable to spend a fair amount of time on this stage, because rushing into a job without due care and forethought can result in disaster halfway through the project, or could lead to an unsatisfactory or unsuccessful end result.

PLANNING STAGE

Having more or less established what you want to achieve with your project, it's time to move on to the planning stage. Sit down with a piece of paper and a pencil and begin to transfer what is in your mind into something visible. It really doesn't matter whether you are an artist or not, as the object of this stage is to get something down on paper as soon as possible. If an idea is left in your mind too long, it might well fade away.

What you put down on paper will depend upon the project you have in mind. If it is a table, you need to ask yourself questions about the height (Is it going to be a coffee table or a dining table?), the type of wood you will be using (Will it fit in with the rest of the furniture in that room?), the type of joints you envisage using (Will you join the boards for the top with biscuits or dowels, and will you enjoy the exercise of constructing proper mortise and tenon joints on the corners, or will you take the easier option of corner dowel joints?).

If you are considering a wall unit or room divider for your lounge or dining room, how big is it going to be and what is the purpose of the unit? Will it need to accommodate a television of a specific size, a set of encyclopaedia or simply a few general books and 'objets d'art'?

As you begin to put a few sketches down on paper, you will usually find that ideas start to flow and your project begins to take on a definite form.

DESIGNING STAGE

One of the most basic facts about any woodworking project is that it is three-dimensional – it has length, width and depth (or height) – and the first piece of information you need is its dimensions.

Rough sketch

Moulding detail

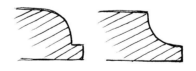

A very basic three-dimensional sketch is really all you need to establish this configuration.

It is also a good idea at this stage to rough-sketch any detail, for example mouldings for edges. If you're not a great artist, 'borrow' designs from a photograph or from a piece that has already been made.

If you design a wall unit, you need to include details such as space for a television, books and maybe even a liquor cabinet (with consideration given to the height of bottles).

With a little experimentation you will find that you can become quite accomplished at sketch planning, which will lead you to the next stage.

DRAWING STAGE

Because all projects are three-dimensional, it is a good idea to complete an accurate scale drawing that shows all three perspectives of the project.

A scale drawing will enable you to obtain the exact dimensions for the thickness, length and width of the wood, as well as the dimensions for any rails and joints. A scale of 1:10 (one-tenth) works well for most items – for large projects, such as wall units, the scale may need to be smaller. A ruler marked with different scales is a useful instrument to own, as it saves you the task of having to calculate these scales all the time. You should also purchase a set square to help get the 90° angles correct. In fact, a school geometry set is an inexpensive

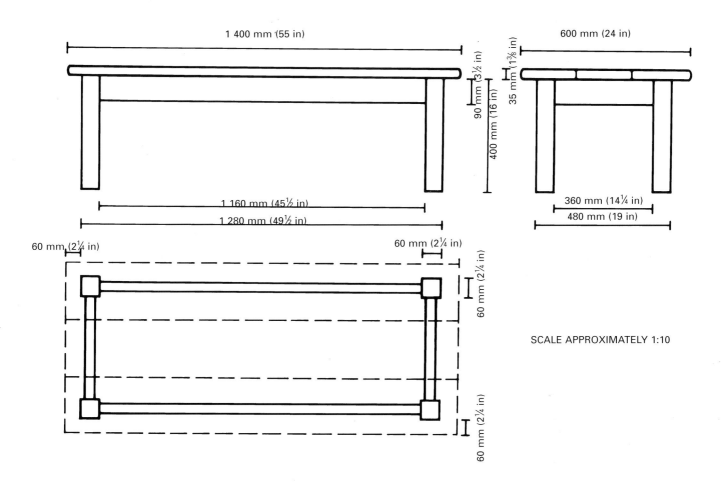

1 400 mm (55 in)

90 mm (3½ in)

400 mm (16 in)

1 160 mm (45½ in)

1 280 mm (49½ in)

60 mm (2¼ in)

60 mm (2¼ in)

60 mm (2¼ in)

60 mm (2¼ in)

600 mm (24 in)

35 mm (1⅜ in)

360 mm (14¼ in)

480 mm (19 in)

SCALE APPROXIMATELY 1:10

and perfectly adequate way of acquiring the drawing tools you will need.

Every project should begin with a drawing like the one above, and it should be to scale so that you can see whether it 'looks' right and that everything fits together. Using this coffee table drawing as an example, you would need to consider how to fix the top to the frame. If you decide to use furniture buttons, you will need another diagram showing the dimensions of these and the slot cut on the inside of the rail (see page 156).

You also need to consider how to fix the rails to the legs. If you choose a haunched mortise and tenon (probably the best joint for this construction), you will need another diagram to calculate these dimensions.

Of course, the more complex the project, the more comprehensive the diagrams will need to be. For example, if the project contains drawers, then each drawer should be drawn individually to enable you to accurately calculate the size of the dovetails on the corner joints.

When you are completely satisfied with your drawings, the next stage is to calculate the size and quantity of the wood and any other materials you may need.

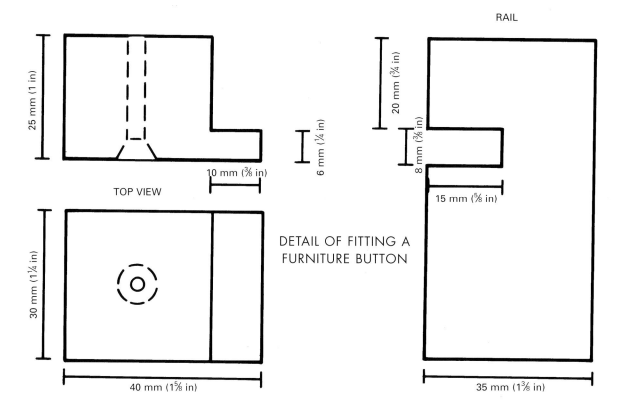

25 mm (1 in)

TOP VIEW

30 mm (1¼ in)

40 mm (1⅝ in)

10 mm (⅜ in)

6 mm (¼ in)

DETAIL OF FITTING A
FURNITURE BUTTON

RAIL

20 mm (¾ in)

8 mm (⅜ in)

15 mm (⅝ in)

35 mm (1⅜ in)

*A complete material list will ensure
that your project flows smoothly
from commencement to completion.*

ORDERING MATERIAL

An accurate and detailed cutting list is invaluable when it comes to identifying and listing each piece of wood and any other materials that you will need for your project. Again using the coffee table as an example, the cutting list would be made up as follows:

Important note
The sizes in a cutting list indicate the finished size. This allows for the additional length required when making any joints, such as those used in the rails. Using the coffee table illustrated on page 155 as an example, when the long rail is fitted into the legs it appears to be 1 160 mm (45½ in) in length. You will, however, need a piece of wood that is 1 240 mm (49 in) long to construct this rail, as you must provide the extra length for the tenons. Although this is a cutting list, it is advisable to be a little generous in the sizes you buy – it's not too difficult

Cutting list for coffee table

Top
- Boards (3) oak: 1 400 x 200 x 35 mm (55 x 8 x 1⅜ in) thick.

Legs
- Boards (4) oak: 400 x 60 x 60 mm (16 x 2¼ x 2¼ in) thick.

Frame
- Rails (2): 1 240 x 90 x 35 mm (49 x 3½ x 1⅜ in) thick.
- Rails (2): 440 x 90 x 35 mm (17½ x 3½ x 1⅜ in) thick.

Additional materials
- Furniture buttons (3 for each long rail + 2 for each short rail = 10).
- Screws (10): No. 8, 40 mm (1⅝ in) brass countersunk
- Sandpaper (coarse to fine)
- 1 litre polyurethane varnish
- 1 x 50 mm (2 in) brush
- Turpentine (mineral spirits)

to cut a piece of wood down to size, but it's virtually impossible to make it any longer if you buy a board that is too short!

When you have made up your cutting list, all that remains for you to do is to take a trip down to your favourite timberyard and carefully select the most appropriate wood for your project before commencing construction. Never be in a hurry when making this selection as the final appearance of your project depends upon the initial choice of the wood.

A FEELING FOR DESIGN AND FORM

The design of most projects is dependent upon what it will be used for and where it will be placed. Although there is no set formula for the proportions used in furniture design, the real secret is to ensure that the piece fits well into the environment for which it was designed, and that it is pleasing to the eye.

Certain pieces of furniture, however, will be governed by certain dimensions. For practical reasons, the top of a kitchen or dining table cannot be any lower than 750 mm, and a desk cannot have knee-room any less than 600 mm from floor to underside.

In other pieces of purpose-built furniture certain factors will have to be considered. To fit a television into a wall unit you will need to know the height, the width and the depth of the television to be used. Incidentally, furniture designers are positioning televisions as close to the ground as possible, as they maintain that this is the most comfortable angle from which they can be viewed.

If you build a desk for your computer, the positioning and size of the various components is very important. For example, a printer needs space to allow paper to be fed into it as well as come out of it, so you cannot place this in a narrow, sealed-off compartment.

Design trends and innovations will also affect the design of your furniture. Commercially produced metal drawer runners now make it possible to construct storage units with large drawers that can move very easily because of the design of the runners.

But more than anything else, the furniture and objects you produce will be an expression of your creativity. Don't be afraid to tackle an ambitious project – just give yourself plenty of time, think carefully through the stages and treat each stage as a separate job. And don't be afraid to create a radical design – if it satisfies your creative urge, then that's fantastic. After all, the hobby of woodworking is primarily about personal enjoyment and satisfaction. And if you do produce a disaster, remember that, although it's sad to waste a beautiful piece of wood, wood is also flammable. Many of my personal disasters have ended up warming the lounge rather than gracing it!

FULL-SIZE TEMPLATE FOR TURNED TRIPOD TABLE LEG (PROJECT ONE)

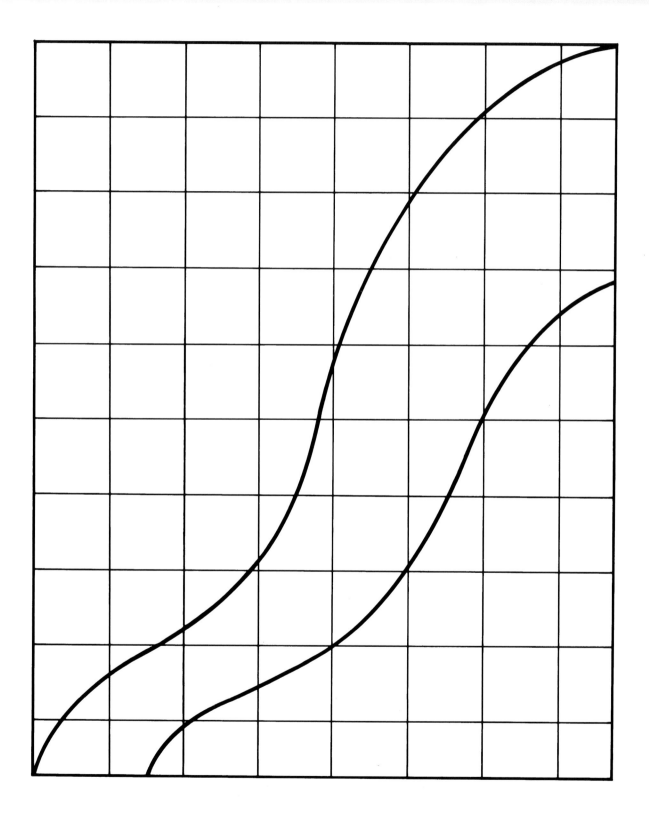

index

Page numbers referring to those with diagrams are in **bold** text and those with photographs in *italic* text